BARIATRIC AIR FRYER

COOKBOOK

1500-Day Quick, Easy, and Mouthwatering Recipes to Take Care of Your New Stomach and Keep the Weight

Off. Live Slimmer and Healthier without Sacrificing Taste. Includes 30-Day Meal Plan

Melissa Jordon

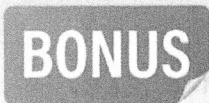

**ANTI-INFLAMMATORY
COOKBOOK FOR BEGINNERS**

1200 Days of Simple Recipes to Heal
the Immune System, Live Healthy
and Reduce your Body
Inflammation

MELISSA JORDON

THIS BOOK INCLUDES A
FREE BONUS

The "Anti-Inflammatory cookbook for beginners" is **100% FREE**, and all you need
to get it is a name and an email address. **It's super simple !**

TO DOWNLOAD THE BONUS SCAN
THE QR CODE BELOW OR GO TO

https://melissajordon.me/download-bonus-ba/

SCAN ME

Table of Contents

Introduction

Maintaining a healthy weight improves the quality of life and enables us to perform our daily activities quickly and comfortably.

Losing a significant excess weight also lowers the risk of obesity-related health conditions, including high cholesterol and blood pressure, type 2 diabetes, and obstructive sleep apnea.

Undergoing bariatric surgery is one way to address obesity. Several bariatric surgery options include gastric sleeve surgery, gastric bypass surgery, and gastric banding.

Regardless of type, the procedure involves removing or reducing the size of your stomach. Bariatric surgery results in rapid weight loss in two ways. You will feel full and stop eating sooner due to your significantly smaller stomach. This translates into a fewer intake of calories. Moreover, there will be a significant drop in the levels of the hunger hormone "ghrelin" in your stomach, so you will not be as hungry compared to your pre-surgery state.

Within 18 to 24 months, most people who had bariatric surgery can expect to shed off at least 50 percent of their excess body weight. Some people would even lose up to 60 or 70 percent. This is highly possible by staying committed to the recommended diet and exercise plan from your surgery team.

The air fryer is a healthier cooking option that you can explore in making surgery-safe meals. This handy kitchen gadget will help you keep a healthy diet without unnecessary stress and complications. This cookbook contains easy-to-follow recipes that are tasty and effective in keeping a healthy weight after bariatric surgery.

CHAPTER 1: Basics of Sleeve Gastrectomy

Difference Between Gastric Sleeve And Gastric Bypass

GASTRIC SLEEVE

GASTRIC BYPASS

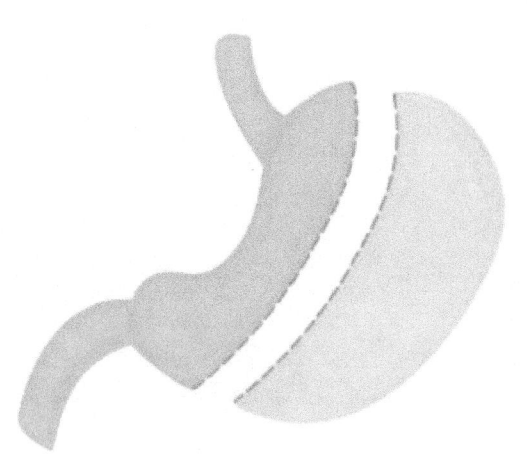

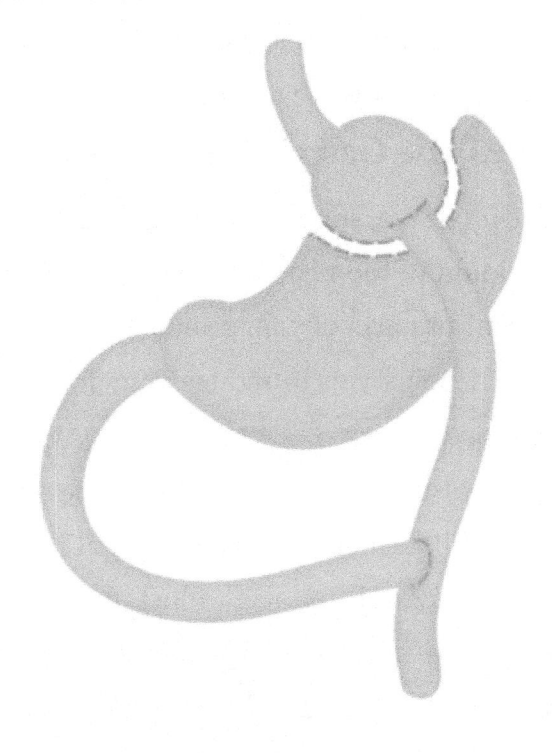

There is a difference between the gastric sleeve and the gastric bypass. The gastric sleeve can be an alternative to a bypass, but there are many different procedures, and each procedure will come with additional risks. The gastric sleeve does not take off any of the weight from your stomach, and it typically takes up to 6 months to lose it. With the bypass, you remove an entire part of your stomach through an incision in your abdomen, which also takes six months to 2 years for you to lose all of the excess weight that would have been put on without surgery.

The gastric sleeve and the bypass operate in different ways, and it is essential to consider the differences because they will determine how much weight you lose and how soon your excess weight will be removed from your body.

There are many positives and negatives to consider when making this decision. The main positive thing about the bypass is that it removes your weight altogether. There is no way that your weight can return or build up in your stomach like with the gastric sleeve. The weight will be gone for good.

When you consider having a bypass, there are also many negative aspects. One of these aspects is that there is a much higher risk of complications because the surgery comes with having to cut open your abdomen and make an incision to remove part of your stomach. An incision also means that there is a higher possibility of infections and the possibility of having significant complications.

If you want to have a gastric sleeve, there are some things that you need to think about first before going ahead with the surgery. It is a good idea to learn all the risks and complications associated with the procedure to make an informed decision about which procedure is proper for you.

In summary, there are some good and some bad things about both procedures, so you must carefully weigh your options before making a decision.

How Does The Gastric Sleeve Work?

After gastric sleeve surgery, your stomach is holding a smaller amount of food because, during surgery, about 75 to 80 percent of parts of your stomach are removed from your body. It helps you to reduce your food carving and weight loss process.

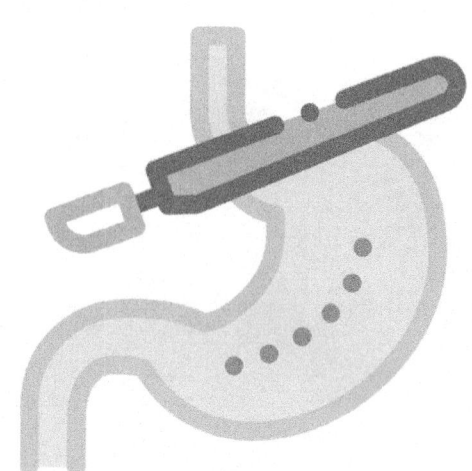

The surgery also removes the part of the stomach that produces Ghrelin. Gherlin is one of the gut hormones your stomach produces; it is also called hunger hormones. Removing these hormones from your body will reduce your hunger feeling and also help to reduce your appetite. By eliminating these hormones from your stomach, you can easily lessen your weight.

Benefits Of Gastric Sleeve Bariatric Surgery

By now, you should have a good idea if you are a candidate for gastric sleeve surgery and how the procedure works. Let's explore some of the benefits the gastric sleeve has to offer.

Significant Weight Loss

Losing significant weight when other non-surgical methods have failed is one of the critical benefits gastric sleeve offers. According to a long-term study of the gastric sleeve, excess weight loss of 60-70% has been recorded by the end of the first year of surgery.

It's Permanent

Once the gastric sleeve is done, you don't have to worry about adjusting like the gastric band. Although it is permanent, revisions and conversions are still possible, just in case you need additional correction after surgery.

No Foreign Objects

The gastric sleeve will not leave any foreign objects (such as silicone) that the gastric band does.

Relatively Safe

The gastric sleeve is a relatively safe procedure with a 30-day mortality rate of 0.08% after surgery. It is safer than gastric bypass and other methods such as gallbladder and hip replacement surgery.

Combats Hunger

Being a restrictive surgery, the gastric sleeve limits the amount of food you can eat at any time. Thus, less food will exert pressure on your stomach, making you full faster. In addition, the part of the stomach removed by the sleeve procedure also removes hormone-producing cells that will make you achieve satiety more quickly and combat hunger.

Minimally Invasive

As of 2020, this procedure is typically done as a laparoscopic procedure. Anywhere from 1 to 5 small incisions are performed to minimize scarring and promote faster healing than open/traditional surgery.

No Rerouting of Your Anatomy

One of the reasons that this procedure is safer; there is no rerouting of the anatomy as observed in other bariatric procedures such as the duodenal switch or the gastric bypass. The additional benefit is that you lower rerouting risks, such as malabsorption and dumping syndrome.

Obesity-Related Diseases Are Improved or Resolved

A gastric sleeve can provide long-term weight loss, which can improve or resolve many obesity-related conditions such as:

- Type 2 diabetes
- Hypertension (high blood pressure)
- Dyslipidemia (high cholesterol)
- Sleep apnea
- GERD
- Asthma
- Reduce your risk of heart disease
- Stroke
- Infertility
- And reducing the risk of future obesity-related diseases

Reliable with a long track record

The first gastric sleeve was performed over three decades ago. As of 2020, millions of gastric sleeves have been performed worldwide and continue to be the most popular bariatric surgery due to the long track record and many case studies that show the long-term reliability of this procedure.

Sleeve Gastrectomy Risks

The gastric sleeve is major surgery. Being a surgical procedure, it has the standard risks that all surgery has, which include internal bleeding, blood clots, infections, stroke, heart attack, allergic reaction to anesthesia, and death. However, the death rate from the gastric sleeve is much lower compared to other surgical procedures at around 0.08%. Let's explore some additional risks and complications related to gastric sleeve.

Leaks

Since a large portion of your stomach is removed, there is a risk of leakage along the staple line. Gastric juices can leak into the abdominal cavity, which can be life-threatening. Pain is the most telltale symptom of a gastric leak. More noticeably, the pain will continue to intensify rather than resolve itself. Other symptoms may include fever, shortness of breath, fast heart rates, and dizziness. Contact your surgeon immediately if you experience pain that does not disappear after surgery. Emergency surgery will be necessary to fix the leak. The percentage of leaking is, on average, 2.8%.

Stricture

One of the most common symptoms of a stricture (the narrowing of the sleeve) is excessive nausea and/or vomiting, making it difficult for food to pass through your digestive tract. Strictures can be diagnosed with a barium swallow along with x-rays and endoscopies. Once diagnosed, it may be resolved with additional surgery to reopen the passageway or convert from a gastric sleeve to a gastric bypass.

Dumping Syndrome

Dumping syndrome (also known as rapid gastric emptying) is a condition that can develop after sleeve surgery. It occurs when food, especially sugar, moves from your stomach into your small bowel too quickly, causing nausea, diarrhea, cramps, stomach pains, or vomiting shortly after eating.

Sleeve Irritation / GERD

Shortly after eating, if you feel pain, you may have an irritation in the gastric lining. You will notice this happens when you eat or drink acids, such as tomatoes or coffee. Usually, PPI (proton pump inhibitors) drugs are taken to resolve the symptoms.

Ulcer

An ulcer can occur after gastric sleeve surgery. Symptoms include dark and tar-like stools that are very foul-smelling. If you exhibit these symptoms, you may have a bleeding ulcer requiring an endoscopy procedure.

Vitamin Deficiencies

Although the gastric sleeve is not a malabsorptive procedure like the gastric bypass or the duodenal switch, nutritional deficiencies can occur due to lower food intake. Supplements should be taken to reduce these deficiencies. The accessories that I recommend to my patients are as follows:

- 1200 mg Calcium Citrate each day (example: 2 Ultra Tums)
- 500-1000 mcg oral B12 or sublingual B12 each day
- 325mg ferrous fumarate, crushable tablets with Vitamin C once per week
- Chewable Flintstones vitamins 2x a day or Vista Vitamin capsules 4x day
- B complex after the first six months
- Flax Seed Oil 1-2 capsules/day
- Zinc and Biotin to minimize hair loss

There are also bariatric vitamin suppliers who specialize in supplements for individuals that had bariatric surgery. Ask your doctor or nutritionist to see what accessories are required before surgery so that when you have surgery, you will be prepared.

Weight regain or unsuccessful weight loss

While this is rare, the gastric sleeve can fail for a small group of individuals. This typically happens when dietary and exercise advice is not followed. There are also ways to cheat the gastric sleeve, for example drinking high-calorie drinks. Sometimes the surgeon may recommend conversion to a more invasive procedure such as a gastric bypass or duodenal switch. In the next chapter, we will explore what needs to be done to get the most out of your gastric sleeve.

CHAPTER 2: Steps and Strategies for Success

Before The Surgery

If you have not yet had your surgery, there are some things you can do ahead of time that will help you during those painful days.

Change your diet.

You must prepare your body for this procedure by going on a high-protein, liquid diet one or two weeks before your surgery. This will shrink your liver, making the surgery safer for you.

Change your grocery list.

You need to have many protein-rich liquids before and after surgery. You will consume clear liquids immediately after surgery for a day or two. After that phase, you will advance to protein shakes and pureed food.

Get the clothes you will need.

You will need transition clothes for the various weights that you will be. You will want your initial clothing after the surgery to fit loosely. You will also want slip-on shoes so you won't have to bend over to tie your shoes.

Stop smoking.

Surgeons take smoking seriously. Before surgery, they will likely give you a blood test to see whether you have been smoking lately. If you have, they will cancel your surgery. Why? If you are smoke-free, your recovery will be quicker. You will need to quit smoking one month before your surgery.

Pack your hospital bag.

You will stay at the hospital for one night, so pack whatever you need for one night.

Prepare your support group.

You will need both physical and mental support after your surgery. You need to educate people before your surgery and line volunteer up who can help you while you recover.

Get your insurance or other financing source ready.

Your health insurance may not pay for this kind of surgery. Typically, body mass index and other health issues are involved. Get the financials ready to pay for your surgery.

Get ahead of the household chores and shopping before surgery.

Make lots of smoothies (minus the ice cubes), cook and freeze meals, clean the house, and do all the laundry before you go in for surgery so that nobody has to do those things later. Buy the stool softeners, over-the-counter medications, and your prescriptions (if possible) ahead of time.

Your friends and family may help you, but it would be easier for everyone if you had most of the work done ahead of time. You will also be sure not to lack anything while at a disadvantage.

Get the facts.

Talk to your surgeon about any concerns or questions about your surgery to understand what will be done and be less anxious about your surgery.

Study up on proteins.

You will need to consume much protein after your surgery. You need to try protein powders to discover which ones you like among the ones that won't add many calories. Food sources are peanut butter, legumes, chicken, meats, and protein shakes.

After The Surgery

Follow your doctor's prescribed diet.

Eat what your doctor tells you to eat after your surgery, which will contain much liquid. If you eat regular food too early or sugary or fat food, you may damage your stomach or harm yourself.

Skip work until you have healed.

Depending on which kind of surgery you have and what type of work you do, you could return to work as soon as two weeks after surgery if you do not lift anything heavy.

Exercise when you can.

Wait about four weeks before you exercise or lift weights to decrease the chance of getting a hernia in the wound.

Go to your check-ups.

Let your doctor check on your progress at the scheduled times. He'll see whether or not you are on schedule with your weight loss goals.

Continue to find suitable foods you can eat.

You need to try out new recipes to stay on your diet plan. You don't want boredom with your food to turn you back to your old eating habits.

Take multivitamins.

It will be hard to get all the nutrition you need from your food significantly less, so be sure to take a multivitamin daily.

Know when to ask for help.

Right after your surgery, it will be hard to get anything done. Hopefully, you got your chores done, groceries and meds purchased, food pre-made and frozen, and your helpers lined up before surgery. Don't be afraid to call on the friends and family who agreed to help you when you need them, especially if you notice a complication.

Follow your prescription.

Keep taking your prescribed medication for as long as you are supposed to. Don't get off of it early. Make an appointment with your doctor if you have discomfort beyond normal.

Count the calories.

You will lose weight if you keep your calorie intake between 600 and 800 daily. Consult your doctor for his suggested calorie target. Don't eat high-calorie food, especially those with sugar and fat.

Don't drink your calories.

Drink water, unsweetened ice tea, and sugar-free juice. You will need to use up your daily allotment of calories on food that contains protein instead of drinks with "empty calories."

Nutritional Concern

After surgery, you must follow specific nutritional guidelines to ensure your body receives what it needs for healing. You will also need to limit some nutrients like sugar and fat that may trigger negative symptoms in your newly altered digestive system, including nausea, vomiting, diarrhea, and abdominal pain. Each nutrient has specific functions and guidelines in your post-operative diet.

a. Protein

Protein is a vital nutrient to consume before but especially after surgery to help preserve lean muscle mass and assist with healing. During each post-op stage, you will slowly increase your daily protein intake as you can tolerate more volume at each meal.

- LIQUID PHASE: 50 to 70 grams daily
- PURÉED FOODS: 50 to 70 grams daily
- SOFT FOODS: 60 to 80 grams daily
- GENERAL FOODS: 60 to 100 grams daily

Research shows that those who have had bariatric surgery should follow a high-protein diet with foods that contain about 35 percent of calories from protein. For a 1,000-calorie diet, typical of the early stages post-op, you will consume foods containing about 350 calories from protein. Since each gram of protein contains about four calories, this comes out to about 87.5 grams of protein, which is within the range of what is recommended for optimal health post-op.

b. Fat

The post-op guidelines for fat intake apply universally throughout the texture stages. Those who have had sleeve gastrectomy or Roux-en-Y surgery should consume no more than 20 percent of their calories from fat. Therefore, if you follow a 1,000-calorie diet, you should consume no more than 200 calories from fat each day. One gram of fat is equal to 9 calories. You should stick to about 22 grams of fat daily for this calorie amount.

This lower fat intake will help prevent weight gain over the long term and reduce the risk for fat intolerance symptoms such as abdominal pain, diarrhea, and nausea. To stay within this limit, try to stick to no more than 5 grams of fat per serving per meal.

c. Carbohydrate

Research shows that those who have had sleeve gastrectomy or Roux-en-Y surgery should consume between 35 percent and 48 percent of their calories from carbohydrates daily.

After bariatric surgery, you will have to follow a reasonably low-carbohydrate diet that does not exceed 130 grams of carbohydrates daily. Research shows you should consume about 40 percent of your calories from carbohydrates for optimal, long-term weight loss success. For example, if you consume 1200 calories daily, you should consume no more than 40 percent, or 480 calories, from carbohydrates daily. Each gram of carbohydrate is equal to about four calories, so that comes out to about 120 grams of carbohydrates daily.

d. Sugar

After bariatric surgery, you should limit sugar as much as possible to reduce the risk of "dumping syndrome," which can cause uncomfortable symptoms such as nausea, vomiting, diarrhea, and abdominal pain. The American Society for Metabolic and Bariatric Surgery recommends that post-op patients consume foods that contain no more than 15 grams of sugar per serving.

Be sure to limit sugar alcohol intake to 10 grams per serving. Sugar alcohols include ingredients such as xylitol, maltitol, and sorbitol. Although they are found in sugar-free products, they can cause uncomfortable digestive symptoms if consumed in excess.

e. Minerals And Other Nutrients

Because your overall consumption is limited after surgery, supplements of vitamins, minerals, and other nutrients are encouraged to bolster the small quantities available in your diet. For all post-op phases, it is recommended that you consume:

- A multivitamin
- Calcium (at least 1,200 milligrams per day)
- Vitamin D (about 1,000 International Units per day)
- Vitamin B12 (500 to 1,000 micrograms per day)

This is not a final list because your doctor may recommend you take other daily supplements if you have or are at greater risk for specific nutrient deficiencies.

f. Keep Hydrated!

After surgery, it will be vital to consume plenty of fluids to help maintain hydration. This may be challenging since your stomach will hold much less than it did before surgery. The guidelines for post-op liquid consumption are 48 to 64 ounces daily during both clear and complete liquid phases and 64 or more ounces, as tolerated, during the puréed, soft, and general food phases. Following the guidelines when planning your fluid intake after bariatric surgery is essential to avoid digestive discomfort.

- Do not drink fluids 30 minutes before and 30 minutes after eating.
- Do not consume carbonated drinks or chew gum since both can allow air to enter the pouch of your stomach, which can cause pain and discomfort.
- Avoid using straws after bariatric surgery since they can cause air to enter the pouch. This can lead to abdominal pain and take up space in your smaller stomach that you need for your new high-protein diet.
- Drink slowly with small sips of no more than an ounce or two. It can help to have a water bottle marked with measurements on the side so you can keep track of how much you are drinking each time you drink and your total intake throughout the day.

Exercise Guidelines For Each Phase of Weight-Loss Surgery

Starting an exercise routine is an excellent idea before having surgery to lose a few extra pounds and make you stronger and feel healthier. You don't have to go overboard and do intense exercise every day, something simple like walking, gardening, yoga, or riding your bicycle is sufficient. Some surgeons may require an exercise routine before having surgery. As with any exercise routine, always ask for your doctor's approval before going on a new exercise regimen to ensure you are healthy enough to do certain physical activities.

Week 1 To 2:
- Walk for about 5 to 10 minutes at least three times per day

Week 3 To 4:
- Walk for about 20 to 30 minutes, with 5 to 10 minutes of gentle stretching

Week 5 To 8:
- Walk for about 20 to 30 minutes, with 5 to 10 minutes of gentle stretching

Week 9 And So On:
- cardiovascular exercise for about 30 to 45 minutes, plus 5 to 10 minutes of gentle stretching
- light to moderate resistance exercises for about 15 to 20 minutes, plus 5 to 10 minutes of gentle stretching
- cardiovascular exercise for about 45 minutes, 5 to 10 minutes of gentle stretching

- light to moderate resistance exercises for about 20 to 30 minutes, 5 to 10 minutes of gentle stretching

Gastric Sleeve Pouch Reset

It is a quick, safe, and natural solution and less invasive than bariatric revision surgery. Specifically, it is a condensed version of the post-op diet and its steps.

Consider the Pouch Reset in case:

- Your weight loss has stopped (You have reached a stalemate)
- You have gained weight
- You are concerned that your sleeve has "stretched"
- You have stopped monitoring your food intake
- You would like to regain control over your diet
- You are eating more than you were prescribed
- You don't know where to start

a. Reset Diet Plan

Here is a comprehensive diet plan for your gastric sleeve reset:

- Day 1: Represents the most changeling phase before returning to eating solid foods. On this day, drink only clear liquids throughout the day (Water; Tea and Unsweetened Drinks; Broth)
- Day 2: You can take denser protein-based liquids (tip: use protein powder in protein shakes + vegetable soup)
- Day 3: Soft solids (2 soft protein sources in addition to shakes and vegetable soups)
- Day 4: Repeat the same diet as Day 3 but with firm solids (also add fat sources like 15 almonds)
- Day 5: Same as Day 4, and here the protein can be any lean protein

b. The Phases

A gastric diet is one of the strict diet plans followed before and after gastric sleeve surgery. It strictly reduces the intake of calories and carbohydrates. These calories and carbohydrates come from sweets, pasta, and potatoes. During a gastric sleeve diet, you must consume liquid foods that are low in calories and high in protein. Protein helps to maintain your muscle mass and also helps to keep your body's energy level. Before two days of surgery, you have to switch to a clear liquid diet, such as a sugar-free protein shake, decaffeinated coffee or tea, sugar-free popsicles, broth, and water. During the gastric sleeve diet, altogether avoid caffeinated and carbonated beverages.

After gastric sleeve surgery, a person must follow a strict diet to recover her body and adjust to the smaller size of her stomach. The person with gastric sleeve surgery eats smaller and more frequent meals for the rest of their lives. The diet plan can be divided into four stages

c. Stage One Diet: Clear Liquids

This stage begins in the first week after your gastric sleeve surgery. In this diet stage, only a few ounces of food drinks have been allowed. This will help your stomach heal without getting stretched by food. The liquid diet includes:

- Water
- Thin soup and broth
- Skim milk
- Decaffeinated coffee and tea
- Sugar-free gelatin and popsicles
- Unsweetened juice

Avoid sugary liquids during the first week of gastric sleeve surgery. Consuming sugary drinks may lead to raising digestive problems and occurs adverse side effects during the surgery. Also, avoid carbonated and caffeinated beverages. During the first week of surgery, always keep your body hydrated; just remember only drink a small amount of liquid at a time.

d. Stage Two Diet: Protein-Rich Liquids

Stage two begins after five days of gastric sleeve surgery. During this stage, you have to allow consuming protein-rich shakes and more liquids like Skimmed milk and unsweetened and blended fruit juice. During this stage, you experience increasing your appetite but have to stick to your diet plan for a positive result. The protein-rich liquid includes:

- Sugar-free protein shakes
- Thin creamed soup and broth
- Non-fat sugar-free puddings
- Low-carb yogurt
- Split pea or lentil soup
- All food in stage one

During stage two, it recommends you to consume about 3 liters of liquid diet per day. Avoid sugary and carbonated liquids during stage two.

e. Stage Three Diet: Puree

Stage three begins after two weeks of gastric sleeve surgery. It allows you to include pureed soft food into your diet. The foods like mashed potatoes, fat-free yogurts, thick and smooth soups, and baked beans. You can eat these diets in small quantities about 4 to 5 times daily. Food allowed during stage three is:

- Puree no-sugar-added fruits.
- Tofu.
- Pureed peas and lentils.
- Eggs.
- Plain yogurt.
- Steamed or boiled vegetables.

f. *Stage Four Diet: Solid Food*

 Stage four begins after four weeks of gastric sleeve surgery. It allows you to take soft solid food into your diet. Try to consume protein-rich foods because it recommends that you should consume at least 60 grams of protein in your daily meal. At this stage, your stomach should be fit to handle solid food. During this stage, you can consume three meals with some snacks. The solid foods allowed in this stage are:

- Lentil and beans soup.
- Hot cereals.
- Fish
- Boil potatoes
- Soft fruits without skin
- Low-fat cheese
- Lean ground turkey, chicken, beef, and pork.
- Cooked vegetables

During this stage, you should avoid whole milk products, snacks, sugary drinks, fibrous vegetables like broccoli, celery, asparagus, starchy foods like white potatoes, pasta and bread, spicy foods, processed foods, fried fast foods, etc.

Top 15 Tips From A Dietician

A correct diet, the necessary precautions, and a healthy lifestyle are perfect allies after a bariatric operation. Therefore, it is essential to follow the following 15 dietary guidelines to face the phase after the process in the most serene way possible and without disturbances.

1. In the early post-surgery period, it is advisable to ingest food and drinks always at a lukewarm temperature so as not to inflame the stomach.
2. Do not drink during meals or the following hour to not fill the gastric pouch quickly.

3. Cut food into small pieces and chew carefully.

4. Eat slowly, stopping when your stomach is full.

5. Do not lie down immediately after eating.

6. Divide meals into three main meals and two snacks. For a good diet, it is necessary to eat little but often. For this reason, it will be essential to maintain three to five meals a day.

7. Limiting excitatory, carbonated, and alcoholic beverages and limiting simple sugars can help you avoid taking in excess calories.

8. Take time to eat. This is fundamental because, before surgery, patients used to eat in a hurry, a habit harmful to digestion. The meal should last at least 20-30 minutes.

9. White meat should be preferred over red meat because they are less fibrous and more digestible.

10. Use raw vegetables (carrots, celery, fennel, etc.) as snacks rather than sweets, junk food, or fattening cookies. If you don't eat vegetables in one meal, remember to increase the number of vegetables in the next meal.

11. The condiment preferred is extra virgin olive oil, in the doses expressly recommended. Avoid the excessive consumption of oily fruits such as nuts, hazelnuts, almonds, or peanuts.

12. Initially, exclude foods that are difficult to digest.

13. Drink 1.5 liters of water per day and always stay away from meals. Especially after bariatric surgery, water plays an essential role. Remember to drink slowly.

14. Bariatric patients need the proper protein intake. For this reason, it is essential to prefer foods with high protein content and choose the right supplement to provide the body with all the proteins it needs.

15. Taking supplements and supplementing the diet with multivitamins Bariatric patients undergo significant transformations, which alter the normal assimilation of all nutrients, so it will be necessary for the post-operative phase to integrate all that the body can no longer absorb with food.

Bariatric Kitchen

Your kitchen is one of your most potent weapons before and after surgery. It can support your goals and defend your weaknesses. How often have you told yourself, "I didn't plan to eat the ice cream, but it was in the house, and I had a moment of weakness"? Before surgery, clean your cupboards to keep your kitchen safe from temptations. That way, even if you want to reach for something indulgent, you won't be able to.

When preparing your bariatric kitchen, stock up on some staples to make life easier or less expensive:

- Almond flour
- Canned beans (garbanzo, pinto, black)
- Canned tuna, chicken, or salmon
- Dried lentils
- Dried spices and herbs
- Eggs
- Extra-virgin olive oil
- Frozen fruit
- Frozen meat
- Frozen vegetables
- Low-sodium chicken broth
- Nuts and seeds
- Old-fashioned oats
- Plain pasta sauce
- Quinoa
- Reduced-fat dairy products
- Whole wheat flour

Foods To Avoid After Surgery

a. Foods With Empty Calories

These include sweets, pastries, rice cakes, popcorn, chips, and pretzels. Most of these foods are loaded with sugar and fat may cause dumping syndrome that causes nausea, vomiting, diarrhea, or cold sweats.

b. Dry Foods

You may consider avoiding dry foods until later after the bariatric surgery. Some of these dry foods are nuts, seeds, or granola. Otherwise, you may take cereals softened with low-fat milk.

When the time is right to consume dry foods, try small amounts at a time. If your body doesn't tolerate them, do not be discouraged, you will be able to eat the foods later.

c. Alcohol

Alcohol will take up the space of your little stomach that should be filled with essential nutrients such as proteins, vitamins, and minerals. Moreover, the alcohol absorption tends to be drastic after the bariatric surgery, thus leading to intoxication.

d. Pasta, Bread, And Rice

Avoid pasta, bread, and rice due to their starchy nature, making them hard to swallow. These foods may also block the stoma posing a risk to your health. You don't have to avoid them wholly, but avoiding them in the first phases of your bariatric diet is advisable.

e. Fibrous Vegetables And Fruits

It is advisable to eat nutritious foods such as vegetables and fruits. However, avoiding fibrous vegetables such as corn, celery, and broccoli is wise.

f. High-Fat Food

Fatty foods such as sausage, bacon, whole milk, and butter will make you nauseous or cause dumping syndrome. Instead, consume low-fat meat, poultry, and low-fat cheese.

g. High Sugar And Caffeinated Drinks

While on the bariatric diet, these drinks may lead to dumping syndrome. Caffeine may also cause dehydration. Otherwise, take water, decaffeinated coffee, or other unsweetened beverages.

CHAPTER 3: Liquid Recipes

1. Air Fryer Vegetable Soup

Preparation time: 10 minutes

Cooking time: 20 minutes

Servings: 5

Ingredients:

- 2 tablespoons extra virgin olive oil
- ½ onion, chopped
- ½ green bell pepper, chopped
- 2 cloves garlic, minced
- 1 1/2 cups green cabbage, chopped
- 1 1/2 cups small cauliflower florets
- 1 cup chopped carrots
- ½ cup green beans, cut into small pieces
- 4 cups low-sodium vegetable broth
- 1 can diced tomatoes, no salt added
- 1 bay leaf
- ½ teaspoon salt
- 4 cups of chopped spinach
- 15-ounce cannellini beans, rinsed
- ¼ cup chopped basil

Directions:

1. Place olive oil in the air fryer and set to sauté. Add onions, bell peppers, and garlic, then cook, often stirring, until softening, which will take 2-3 minutes.

2. Put in the carrots, cauliflower, cabbage, and green beans and cook for 4-5 minutes, stirring often.

3. Add the broth, tomatoes, bay leaf, and salt. Turn off the heat, lock the lid, and cook on high for 5 minutes.

4. Release the pressure using quick release, open the lid carefully, and remove the bay leaf. Stir in the spinach, basil, and beans.

5. Ready to serve. You may drizzle more olive oil on top if desired.

Per serving: Calories: 192kcal; Fat: 6.6g; Carbs: 26g; Protein: 7.3g

2. Cheesy Red Bean Soup

Preparation time: 10 minutes

Cooking time: 15 minutes

Servings: 4

Ingredients:

- 1 cup of red beans
- 3 tablespoons of butter
- 1 carrot, roughly chopped
- 1 medium onion, roughly sliced
- 3 garlic cloves, minced
- 3 tablespoons of tomato paste
- ½ cup of half and half
- 4 cups of water
- 2 teaspoons of salt
- 2 pinches of black pepper
- Crunchy tortilla chips to garnish
- ½ cup of Mexican cheese, shredded

Directions:

1. Set the Air fryer to 375 deg. F for 5 minutes, put the garlic, onion, and carrots in the cooking tray.
2. Insert the cooking tray into the Oven when it displays "Add Food."
3. Remove from the Oven when cooking time is complete.
4. Put the butter in a wok and add the garlic mixture, salt, and black pepper. Sauté it for about 3 minutes, stirring the red beans, water, and tomato paste.
5. Secure the wok's lid and cook for 10 minutes on medium heat.
6. Fold in the Mexican cheese and half and half.
7. Serve garnished with crispy tortilla chips.

Per serving: Calories: 418kcal; Fat: 18.5g; Carbs: 49g; Protein: 17.6g

3. Tomato Soup

Preparation time: 15 minutes
Cooking time: 30 minutes
Servings: 6
Ingredients:

- 1/2 tsp of salt
- 6 tomatoes, halved
- 1 tsp of garlic powder
- 1 onion, chopped
- 1 tbsp of olive oil
- 5 cloves of garlic, peeled
- 1/4 cup of light cream
- 1/2 tsp of black pepper

- 1 1/2 cups of chicken broth
- 1 tsp of granulated brown sugar
- 1/4 cup of basil, chopped
- 1/4 cup of parmesan cheese, grated

Directions:

8. Preheat the air fryer to 400 deg. F. Add tomatoes, garlic cloves, and onions to the lined basket.
9. Add brown sugar, salt, olive oil, and black pepper.
10. Blend all the veggies in a food processor.
11. Then add chicken broth, garlic powder, light cream, and parmesan cheese.
12. Cook for about 30 minutes in the air fryer. Serve with extra cheese and basil.

Per serving: Calories: 198kcal; Fat: 7g; Carbs: 12g; Protein: 4g

4. Healthy Bean Soup

Preparation time: 30 minutes
Cooking time: 20 minutes
Servings: 10
Ingredients:

- Cilantro
- 3 tsp of cumin
- 4 tomatoes, diced
- 1/2 cup of water
- 3/4 tsp of sea salt
- 2 jalapenos, diced
- 4 cans of black beans
- 1/4 cup of lime juice
- 1/2 cup of onion, diced
- 2 cups of vegetable broth

- 1/4 cup of cilantro, chopped

Directions:

1. Mix all the veggies and spices in a bowl. Keep in the fridge for about 30 minutes.
2. Add beans, vegetable broth, cumin, and water to a ramekin.
3. Cook for about 10 minutes at 400 deg. F.
4. Also, air fry veggies. Mix everything and cook for 5 minutes.
5. Top with cilantro and serve.

Per serving: Calories: 250kcal; Fat: 8g; Carbs: 44g; Protein: 9g

5. Taco Cheese Soup

Preparation time: 10 minutes

Cooking time: 25 minutes

Servings: 8

Ingredients:

- 1 lb. ground beef
- 1 lb. ground pork
- ½ cup Monterey Jack cheese, grated
- 2 tbsp. parsley, chopped
- 4 cups beef broth
- 20 oz. can tomato
- 16 oz. cream cheese
- 2 tbsp. taco seasonings

Directions:

1. Add the ground meats to the air fryer and sauté for 10 minutes.
2. Add taco seasonings, tomatoes, and cream cheese. Stir to combine.
3. Secure pot with lid and cook on manual high pressure for 15 minutes.

4. Quick release pressure, then opens the lid.
5. Add parsley and stir well. Top with grated cheese and serve.

Per serving: Calories: 445kcal; Fat: 28.1g; Carbs: 5.7g; Protein: 41.1g

6. Mushrooms Mix Veg Broth

Preparation time: 3 minutes

Cooking time: 10 minutes

Servings: 1

Ingredients:

- 4 cups vegetable broth
- 4 mushrooms (sliced)
- ¼ cup Miso paste
- 4 tsp. soy sauce
- ⅓ cup tofu (cubes)
- 2 green onions (sliced)

Directions:

1. Add vegetable broth and mushrooms into the air fryer pot.
2. Mix miso paste, soy sauce, tofu, and green onions.
3. Cook for 10 minutes at 300 deg. F.
4. When ready, serve the delicious side dish!

Per serving: Calories: 115kcal; Fat: 7g; Carbs: 9g; Protein: 40g

7. Kale Beef Soup

Preparation time: 15 minutes
Cooking time: 43 minutes
Servings: 4
Ingredients:

- 1 lb. beef stew meat
- 1 tsp. cayenne pepper
- 3 garlic cloves, crushed
- 4 cups chicken broth
- 2 tbsp. olive oil
- 1 cup kale, chopped
- 1 onion, sliced
- ¼ tsp. black pepper
- ½ tsp. salt

Directions:

1. Add oil into the air fryer and set on Sauté mode.
2. Add garlic and onion. Sauté for 3 minutes.
3. Add meat and sauté for 5 minutes.
4. Add broth and season with cayenne pepper, pepper, and salt. Stir well.
5. Secure pot with lid and cook on manual high pressure for 25 minutes.
6. Quick release pressure, then opens the lid.
7. Add kale and stir well. Sit for 10 minutes.
8. Stir well and serve.

Per serving: Calories: 333kcal; Fat: 15.6g; Carbs: 6.3g; Protein: 40.3g

8. Coconut Lime Soup

Preparation time: 6 minutes
Cooking time: 10 minutes
Servings: 3-4
Ingredients:

- ½ Tbsp of coconut oil
- 1 Finely chopped onion
- 1 tsp of ground coriander powder
- 1 Medium sized Cauliflower that is broken into a large floret
- 3 Cups of Vegetable Broth
- ½ Cup of Coconut Milk
- 2-3 Tbsp of Lime Juice
- 1 Pinch of Salt to taste

Directions:

1. Start by heating the Air fryer and setting the Manual button to sauté mode, and sauté the onion for 6 minutes.
2. Add the coriander and keep stirring for a couple of minutes.
3. Add the rest of the ingredients from the cauliflower, the vegetable broth, and the coconut milk; then, stir the ingredients to combine them.
4. Set the timer to 10 minutes.
5. Once the timer sets off; press the button, keep warm, and release the pressure
6. Blend the ingredients with a blender until it becomes soft
7. Add the lime juice and adjust the salt to taste
8. Serve and enjoy your soup!

Per serving: Calories: 262.8kcal; Fat: 12.7g; Carbs: 16g; Protein: 22g

9. Carrot Soup With Fowl

Preparation time: 8 minutes

Cooking time: 20 minutes

Servings: 4

Ingredients:

- ½ fowl or chicken
- 2 quarts of chicken broth
- ¼ Cup of coarsely chopped onion
- ½ Cup of coarsely chopped carrots
- 1 teaspoon of saffron threads
- 1 tablespoon of fresh chopped parsley
- 1 Cup of cooked egg noodles

Directions:

1. Start by combining all together the stewing chicken or fowl with the chicken broth in your Air fryer
2. Press sauté and add the onions, the carrots, and the saffron
3. Now, close the lid and set it at high pressure for around 20 minutes
4. Once the timer beeps, remove the chicken and shred it from the bone and cut it into small pieces
5. Strain your saffron broth with a fine sieve, and then add the parsley and the cooked noodles to your broth.
6. Return your soup to simmer for a few minutes
7. Serve and enjoy a delicious and nutritious soup

Per serving: Calories: 154.4kcal; Fat: 0.8g; Carbs: 27.2g; Protein: 10.9g

10. Roasted Tomato Soup

Preparation time: 15 min

Cooking time: 30 min

Servings: 6

Ingredients:

- Tomatoes - 6 fresh, halved
- White onion - 1 quartered
- Garlic - 5 cloves, peeled
- Olive oil - 1 tablespoon
- Pepper - ½ teaspoon
- Granulated sugar - 1 teaspoon
- Basil - ¼ cup, chopped
- Chicken broth - 1½ cups
- Salt and pepper - to taste

Directions:

1. Heat the fryer to 400 deg. Add the onions, tomatoes, olive oil, salt, garlic, pepper, and sugar to the basket lined with baking paper.
2. Air fry for 30 minutes until the vegetables are soft. Remember to peel the tomatoes and remove the stems once the vegetables are cooled.
3. Blend the vegetables in a food processor. Add the basil as well.
4. Transfer the vegetable soup to a pot. Pour in the chicken broth and heat.
5. Serve hot!

Per serving: Calories: 198kcal; Fat: 7g; Carbs: 46g; Protein: 19g

11. Basil Tomato Soup

Preparation time: 5 minutes

Cooking time: 15 minutes

Servings: 4

Ingredients:

- 1 onion, roughly sliced
- 1 potato, roughly diced
- ½ cup of tomatoes
- 2 tablespoons of tomato paste
- 2 tablespoons of sun-dried tomatoes
- 1 tablespoon of basil leaves, freshly chopped
- 1 carrot, roughly chopped
- 4 cups of water
- Salt and black pepper to taste
- 2 tablespoons of butter

Directions:

1. Set the Air fryer to 375 deg. F for 5 minutes. Put the tomatoes, potato, carrot, and sun-dried tomatoes in the cooking tray. Insert the cooking tray into the Oven when it displays "Add Food."
2. Remove from the Oven when cooking time is complete. Put the butter in a wok and add the tomato mixture and onions.
3. Sauté it for about 3 minutes, stirring the remaining ingredients. Secure the wok's lid and cook for about 12 minutes on medium heat. Puree the contents of the soup with an immersion blender and serve hot.

Per serving: Calories: 239kcal; Fat: 12.8g; Carbs: 29.6g; Protein: 4.2g

12. Tortilla And White Beans Soup

Preparation time: 10 minutes

Cooking time: 27 minutes

Servings: 4

Ingredients:

- 1 cup of white beans
- 4 tablespoons butter
- ¼ teaspoon white pepper
- 1 onion, roughly sliced
- 1 tablespoon sun-dried tomatoes
- ¼ cup fresh cream
- 4 cups water
- 2 teaspoons salt
- 1 carrot, roughly chopped
- 4 garlic cloves, minced
- 4 tablespoons tomato paste
- Crunchy tortilla chips for garnish

Directions:

1. Put the butter, garlic, carrots, onions, and white pepper in the Air fryer and select "Sauté."
2. Sauté for 5 minutes and add white beans, sun-dried tomatoes, tomato paste, salt, and water.
3. Set the Air fryer to "Soup" and cook for 12 minutes at high pressure.
4. Release the pressure naturally and add sour cream.
5. Blend the contents of the Air fryer to a smooth consistency and top with crunchy tortilla chips.

Per serving: Calories: 353kcal; Fat: 14.7g; Carbs: 44.2gg; Protein: 14g

13. Pepper Beef Stew

Preparation time: 15 minutes
Cooking time: 23 minutes
Servings: 6
Ingredients:

- 10 oz. beef short ribs
- 1 cup chicken stock
- 1 garlic clove
- 3 oz chive stems
- 4 oz. green peas
- ¼ teaspoon salt
- 1 teaspoon turmeric
- 1 green pepper
- 2 teaspoon butter
- ½ teaspoon chili flakes
- 4 oz. kale

Directions:

1. Preheat the air fryer to 360 deg. F.
2. Place the butter in the air fryer basket tray.
3. Add the beef short ribs.
4. Sprinkle the beef short ribs with salt, turmeric, and chili flakes.
5. Cook the beef short ribs for 15 minutes.
6. Meanwhile, remove the seeds from the green pepper and chop them.
7. Chop the kale and dice the chives.
8. When the time is over – pour the chicken stock into the beef short ribs.
9. Add the chopped green pepper and diced chives.
10. After this, sprinkle the mixture with the green peas.
11. Peel the garlic clove and add it to the mixture too.
12. Mix it up using a wooden spatula.
13. Then chop the kale and add it to the stew mixture.
14. Stir the stew mixture and cook it at 360 F for 8 minutes.
15. When the stew is cooked – let it rest a little.
16. Then mix the stew up and transfer to the serving plates.
17. Enjoy!

Per serving: Calories: 144kcal; Fat: 5.8g; Carbs: 7g; Protein: 15.7g

14. Asian Pork Soup

Preparation time: 10 minutes
Cooking time: 30 minutes
Servings: 5
Ingredients:

- 1 lb. ground pork
- 1 tsp. ground ginger
- ¼ cup soy sauce
- 4 cups beef broth
- ½ cabbage head, chopped
- 2 carrots, peeled and shredded
- 1 onion, chopped
- 1 tbsp. olive oil
- Pepper
- Salt

Directions:

1. Add oil into the air fryer and set on Sauté mode.

2. Add meat to the pot and sauté for 5 minutes.
3. Add remaining ingredients and stir well.
4. Secure pot with lid and cook on manual high pressure for 25 minutes.
5. Quick release pressure, then opens the lid.
6. Stir well and serve hot.

Per serving: Calories: 229kcal; Fat: 7.2g; Carbs: 10.6g; Protein: 29.8g

15. Kale Cottage Cheese Soup

Preparation time: 5 minutes
Cooking time: 5 minutes
Servings: 4
Ingredients:

- 5 cups fresh kale, chopped
- 1 tbsp. olive oil
- 1 cup cottage cheese, cut into small chunks
- 3 cups chicken broth
- ½ tsp. black pepper
- ½ tsp. sea salt

Directions:

1. Add all ingredients except cottage cheese into the air fryer and stir well.
2. Secure pot with lid and cook on manual high pressure for 5 minutes.
3. Quick release pressure, then opens the lid.
4. Add cottage cheese and stir well.
5. Serve hot and enjoy.

Per serving: Calories: 152kcal; Fat: 5.6g; Carbs: 11.7g; Protein: 13.9g

16. Onion Soup

Preparation time: 5 minutes
Cooking time: 1 hour
Servings: 4
Ingredients:

- Beef stock - 6 cups
- Butter - 3 tablespoons
- Leaf - 1 bay
- Onions - 6 cups, sliced
- Salt - 1/2 teaspoon
- Soy sauce - 1 teaspoon
- Thyme - 2 teaspoons

Directions:

1. Line the basket with aluminum foil and heat the air fryer to 300 deg. F. Cook onions for 30 minutes, stirring often.
2. In a saucepan over medium heat, cook for 15 min the onions, thyme, butter, soy, and salt. Also, add the bay leaf.
3. Pour in the beef broth and then simmer for 15 min.
4. Remove the bay leaf and blend everything.
5. Serve in soup bowls.

Per serving: Calories: 268kcal; Fat: 8g; Carbs: 25g; Protein: 10g

17. Air Fryer Greek Beef Stew

Preparation time: 15 minutes
Cooking time: 40 minutes
Servings: 4
Ingredients:

- 1 ½ pounds stew beef cut into small cubes

- ¼ cup of butter
- 8 small onions
- 2-3 carrots, sliced
- ¾ cups tomato paste
- 1 teaspoon cinnamon

Directions:

1. Set air fryer to sauté mode and cook beef in the butter until browned. This will take about 5 minutes. Then remove.
2. Put the onions in the pot and sauté for about 5 minutes.
3. Stop sauté mode. Add beef to the pot and carrots, tomato paste, and cinnamon. Add 2-3 cups of water.
4. Lock the lid, set pressure to high, and cook for 35 minutes.
5. Allow the steam to release naturally for 10 minutes and then quickly release the remaining pressure.
6. Ready to serve.

Per serving: Calories: 479kcal; Fat: 20g; Carbs: 31g; Protein: 43g

18. Chicken Rice Noodle Soup

Preparation time: 5 minutes

Cooking time: 10 minutes

Servings: 6

Ingredients:

- 6 cups chicken, cooked and cubed
- 3 tbsp. rice vinegar
- 2 ½ cups cabbage, shredded
- 2 tbsp. fresh ginger, grated
- 2 tbsp. soy sauce
- 3 garlic cloves, minced

- 8 oz. rice noodles
- 1 bell pepper, chopped
- 1 large carrot, peeled and sliced
- 6 cups chicken stock
- 1 onion, chopped
- ½ tsp. black pepper

Directions:

1. Add all ingredients into the air fryer and stir well.
2. Secure pot with lid and cook on manual high pressure for 10 minutes.
3. Quick release pressure, then opens the lid.
4. Stir well and serve.

Per serving: Calories: 306kcal; Fat: 5.1g; Carbs: 18.7g; Protein: 43.1g

19. Air Fryer Fish Stew

Preparation time: 5 minutes

Cooking time: 15 minutes

Servings: 4

Ingredients:

- 4 tablespoons of extra-virgin olive oil
- 1 medium red onion, chopped
- 4 garlic cloves, chopped
- ½ cup of dry white wine
- 8-ounce clam juice
- 2 1/2 cups of water
- 1 1/2 cups of fresh tomatoes with juices
- kosher salt
- black pepper for taste
- pinch of crushed red pepper for taste

- 2 pounds of sea bass cut into 2-inch pieces
- 2 tablespoons lemon juice
- 2 tablespoons of fresh dill, chopped

Directions:

1. Use the sauté setting on your air fryer and cook onions in 2 tablespoons of olive oil for 3 minutes, until golden brown.
2. Add the chopped garlic, and sauté until fragrant.
3. Add the white wine, and scrape up any brown bits until about half of the wine has evaporated.
4. Add the clam juice, water, tomatoes, salt, pepper, and a pinch of crushed red pepper.
5. Turn the sauté off, cover and seal your air fryer, and set it to manual high pressure for 5 minutes.
6. After this, quickly release the pressure.
7. Open the air fryer and turn the saute setting back on. Once the soup is simmering, add the fish pieces, and simmer for about 5 minutes, until the fish flakes apart easily.
8. Turn off saute mode, stir in lemon juice and fresh dill, and the remaining olive oil. Season to taste and serve.

Per serving: Calories: 471kcal; Fat: 20g; Carbs: 24g; Protein: 43g

20. Air Fryer Bean Soup

Preparation time: 20 minutes
Cooking time: 1 hour and 25 minutes
Servings: 6
Ingredients:

- 1 pound of white beans
- 1 ¼ pound of beef shanks with bone
- 1 white onion, chopped
- 1 green bell pepper, chopped
- 2 carrots, chopped
- 4 tablespoons olive oil
- 2 tablespoons fresh parsley, chopped
- ½ teaspoon garlic, minced
- ½ tablespoon salt
- 1 can of tomatoes, diced
- 1-liter water
- 3 bay leaves
- ½ teaspoon paprika

Directions:

1. Immerse beans in a bowl of cold water overnight.
2. Place the beef shanks and olive oil in the air fryer and turn on saute setting. Brown on both sides
3. Remove the beans from the water, and rinse. Add beans, diced tomatoes, paprika, bay leaves, and garlic.
4. Add water, close the lid, and cook on the manual high setting for 1 hour. Make sure the beans are soft, and if not, cook for another 30 minutes. Serve.

Per serving: Calories: 86kcal; Fat: 5g; Carbs: 9.7g; Protein: 2.8g

CHAPTER 4: Breakfast Recipes

21. Muffin Mix Breakfast

Preparation time: 6 minutes

Cooking time: 12 minutes

Servings: 1

Ingredients:

- 1 tbsp. oil
- 1 egg
- Whole wheat muffin
- Black pepper to taste
- 1 cup cheese (shredded)
- 4 slices of Canadian bacon

Directions:

1. Whisk the egg in a bowl.
2. Add black pepper and mix well.
3. Grease the round baking tray with oil and pour the egg mixture.
4. Add cheese and bacon.
5. Place the round baking tray in the air fryer with the muffin.
6. Let it cook for 12 minutes at 300 deg. F.
7. When ready, enjoy!

Per serving: Calories: 90kcal; Fat: 8g; Carbs: 20g; Protein: 25g

22. Mushroom Cheese Salad

Preparation time: 10 minutes

Cooking time: 15 minutes

Servings: 2

Ingredients:

- 10 mushrooms, halved
- 1 tbsp. fresh parsley, chopped
- 1 tbsp. olive oil
- 1 tbsp. mozzarella cheese, grated
- 1 tbsp. cheddar cheese, grated
- 1 tbsp. dried mix herbs
- Pepper
- Salt

Directions:

1. Add all ingredients into the bowl and toss well.
2. Transfer bowl mixture into the air fryer baking dish.
3. Place in the air fryer and then cook at 380 deg. F for 15 minutes.
4. Serve and enjoy.

Per serving: Calories: 90kcal; Fat: 7g; Carbs: 2g; Protein: 5g

23. Cauliflower Mix Black Cod

Preparation time: 6 minutes

Cooking time: 10 minutes

Servings: 1

Ingredients:

- 1 cauliflower (chopped)
- ½ tbsp. vinegar
- Salt to taste
- 1 lb. black cod (chopped)
- For Sauce
- ½ cup milk
- ½ cup cheese
- ½ cup basil

Directions:

1. Add vinegar and salt to the air fryer pot.
2. Mix cauliflower and black cod chopped.
3. Cook at 300 deg. F for 15 minutes.
4. Meanwhile, prepare sauce: mix milk, cheese, and basil.
5. When ready, serve by pouring the sauce over it to enjoy!

Per serving: Calories: 100kcal; Fat: 10g; Carbs: 8g; Protein: 13.1 g

24. Kale With Tuna

Preparation time: 4 minutes

Cooking time: 10 minutes

Servings: 1

Ingredients:

- 12 cups Kale (chopped)
- 2 tbsp. lemon juice
- 1 tbsp. oil
- 1 can of tuna fish
- 1 tbsp. garlic (minced)
- 1 tsp. soy sauce
- Salt and pepper to taste

Directions:

1. Add oil into the air fryer pot.
2. Mix tuna fish, garlic, soy sauce, lemon juice, kale, salt, and pepper.
3. Cook at 300 deg. F for 10 minutes.
4. When ready, enjoy!

Per serving: Calories: 90kcal; Fat: 8g; Carbs: 20g; Protein: 25g

25. Garlic Potatoes With Bacon

Preparation time: 10 minutes

Cooking time: 20 minutes

Servings: 2

Ingredients:

- 4 potatoes, peeled and cut into medium cubes
- 6 garlic cloves, minced
- 4 bacon slices, chopped
- 2 rosemary springs, chopped
- 1 tbsp. olive oil
- Salt and black pepper to taste
- 2 eggs, whisked

Directions:

1. Mix the oil in your air fryer's pan with potatoes, garlic, bacon, rosemary, salt, pepper, and eggs. Whisk.
2. Cook the potatoes at 400 deg. F for 20 minutes, divide everything among plates and serve for breakfast. Enjoy!

Per serving: Calories: 211kcal; Fat: 3g; Carbs: 8g; Protein: 5 g

26. Almond Crust Chicken

Preparation time: 10 minutes

Cooking time: 25 minutes

Servings: 2

Ingredients:

- 2 chicken breasts, skinless and boneless
- 1 tbsp Dijon mustard
- 2 tbsp mayonnaise
- ¼ cup almonds
- Pepper

- Salt

Directions:

1. Add almond into the food processor and process until finely ground.
2. Transfer almonds to a plate and set aside.
3. Mix mustard and mayonnaise and spread over chicken.
4. Coat chicken with almonds, place into the air fryer basket and cook at 350 F for 25 minutes.
5. Serve and enjoy.

Per serving: Calories: 409kcal; Fat: 22g; Carbs: 6g; Protein: 45g

27. Tuna And Spring Onions Salad

Preparation time: 5 minutes
Cooking time: 15 minutes
Servings: 4
Ingredients:

- 14 oz. canned tuna drained and flaked
- 2 spring onions; chopped.
- 1 cup arugula
- 1 tbsp. olive oil
- A pinch of salt and black pepper

Directions:

1. Place all the ingredients except the oil and arugula in a bowl, and whisk.
2. Preheat the air fryer to 360 deg. F, then add the oil to grease the air fryer. Pour the tuna mix, stir well, and cook for 15 minutes.
3. In a salad bowl, combine the arugula with the tuna mix, toss, and serve.

Per serving: Calories: 212kcal; Fat: 8g; Carbs: 5g; Protein: 8 g

28. Simple Egg Breakfast

Preparation time: 4 minutes
Cooking time: 10 minutes
Servings:
Ingredients:

- 4 eggs
- 1 tsp. yellow mustard
- ½ cup mayonnaise
- 2 green onions (chopped)
- ½ tsp. paprika
- Salt and pepper to taste

Directions:

1. Mix eggs, yellow mustard, and green onion in a bowl.
2. Add mayonnaise, salt, and pepper with paprika. Beat well.
3. Add the mixture to a round baking tray.
4. Place it in the air fryer and let it cook for 10 minutes.
5. When ready, serve and enjoy!

Per serving: Calories: 96kcal; Fat: 9g; Carbs: 10g; Protein: 35g

29. Apple Pie

Preparation time: 10 minutes
Cooking time: 13 minutes
Servings: 6
Ingredients:

- 1 egg
- 1 tbsp of water
- 1 pie crust

- 1 tsp of apple pie spice
- 1 tsp of cinnamon sugar
- 1/2 tsp of vanilla extract
- 1 cup of apple pie filling
- 1 1/2 tbsp of caramel sauce

Directions:

1. Mix apple pie filling, caramel sauce, apple pie spice, and vanilla extract in a bowl.
2. Roll out pie crust. Make circles.
3. Make an egg wash by mixing egg & water.
4. Top circles with the egg wash. Place the filling mixture in between each circle. Roll edges to seal them.
5. Set the air fryer to 350°F. Cook pies in it until brown.
6. Top with powdered cinnamon and brown sugar.
7. Serve with caramel sauce and enjoy.

Per serving: Calories: 189kcal; Fat: 8g; Carbs: 26g; Protein: 3g

30. Potatoes With Bacon

Preparation time: 10 minutes

Cooking time: 20 minutes

Servings: 2

Ingredients:

- 4 potatoes, peeled and cut into medium cubes
- 4 bacon slices, chopped
- 2 rosemary springs, chopped
- 1 tablespoon olive oil
- Salt and black pepper to the taste
- 2 eggs, whisked

Directions:

1. Mix oil with potatoes, bacon, rosemary, salt, pepper, and eggs in your air fryer's pan and whisk.
2. Cook potatoes at 400 degrees F for 20 minutes, divide everything between plates, and serve for breakfast. Enjoy!

Per serving: Calories: 211kcal; Fat: 3g; Carbs: 8g; Protein: 5g

31. Garlic Bacon Pizza

Preparation time: 10 minutes

Cooking time: 13 minutes

Servings: 4

Ingredients:

- Cooking spray
- 4 dinner rolls
- 1 cup of tomato sauce
- 4 garlic cloves, minced
- 1/2 tsp of garlic powder
- 6 bacon slices, chopped
- 1/2 tsp of oregano, dried
- 1 1/4 cups of cheddar cheese, shredded

Directions:

1. Spray dinner rolls and place them in the air fryer.
2. Cook for around 2 minutes at 370 deg. F.
3. Add all the ingredients on top and cook for around 8 minutes at 370 deg. F.
4. Serve and enjoy.

Per serving: Calories: 217kcal; Fat: 5g; Carbs: 12g; Protein: 4g

32. Breakfast Fish Tacos

Preparation time: 10 minutes

Cooking time: 13 minutes

Servings: 2

Ingredients:

- 4 big tortillas
- 1 red bell pepper, chopped
- 1 yellow onion, chopped
- 4 white fish fillets, skinless and boneless
- ½ cup salsa
- A handful of mixed romaine lettuce, spinach, and radicchio
- 4 tablespoon parmesan, grated

Directions:

1. Put fish fillets in your air fryer and cook at 350 degrees F for 6 minutes.
2. Meanwhile, heat a pan over medium-high heat, add bell pepper and onion, stir and cook for 1-2 minutes.
3. Arrange tortillas on a working surface, divide fish fillets, spread salsa over them, divide mixed veggies and greens, and spread parmesan on each at the end.
4. Roll your tacos, place them in the preheated air fryer and cook at 350 degrees F for 6 minutes.
5. Divide fish tacos between plates and serve for breakfast. Enjoy!

Per serving: Calories: 200kcal; Fat: 3g; Carbs: 9g; Protein: 5g

33. Shrimp Frittata

Preparation time: 10 minutes

Cooking time: 15 minutes

Servings: 2

Ingredients:

- 4 eggs
- ½ teaspoon basil, dried
- Cooking spray
- Salt and black pepper to the taste
- ½ cup rice, cooked
- ½ cup shrimp, cooked, peeled, deveined, and chopped
- ½ cup baby spinach, chopped
- ½ cup Monterey jack cheese, grated

Directions:

1. Place eggs with salt, pepper, and basil in a bowl, then whisk.
2. Grease your air fryer's pan with cooking spray and add rice, shrimp, and spinach.
3. Add eggs, mix, sprinkle cheese, and cook in your air fryer at 350 degrees F for 10 minutes.
4. Divide among plates and serve for breakfast. Enjoy!

Per serving: Calories: 162kcal; Fat: 6g; Carbs: 8g; Protein: 4g

34. Protein Egg Cups

Preparation time: 10 minutes

Cooking time: 9 minutes

Servings: 2

Ingredients:

- 3 eggs, lightly beaten
- 4 tomato slices
- 4 tsp cheddar cheese, shredded
- 2 bacon slices, cooked and crumbled
- Pepper
- Salt

Directions:

1. Spray silicone muffin molds with cooking spray.
2. In a bowl, whisk the egg with pepper and salt.
3. Preheat the air fryer to 350 F. Pour eggs into the silicone muffin molds.
4. Divide cheese and bacon into molds.
5. Top each with a tomato slice and place in the air fryer basket.
6. Cook for 9 minutes. Serve and enjoy.

Per serving: Calories: 67kcal; Fat: 4g; Carbs: 1g; Protein: 5.1g

35. Air Fried Banana Bites

Preparation time: 5 minutes

Cooking time: 5 minutes

Servings: 2

Ingredients:

- 2 bananas
- Avocado oil spray

Directions:

1. Cut the bananas into equal sizes.

2. Preheat the Ninja air fryer to 375 deg. F.
3. Put the banana bites in the air fryer basket.
4. Spray avocado oil. Cook in the air fryer for about 5 minutes until they get brown.
5. Serve and enjoy.

Per serving: Calories: 107kcal; Fat: 0.7g; Carbs: 27g; Protein: 1.3g

36. Lemony Raspberries Bowls

Preparation time: 5 minutes

Cooking time: 12 minutes

Servings: 2

Ingredients:

- 1 cup raspberries
- 2 tbsp. butter
- 2 tbsp. lemon juice
- 1 tsp. cinnamon powder

Directions:

1. In your air fryer, mix all the ingredients.
2. Toss, cover, and cook at 350 deg. F for 12 minutes, divide into bowls and serve for breakfast.

Per serving: Calories: 208kcal; Fat: 6g; Carbs: 14g; Protein: 3g

37. Mushrooms And Cheese Spread

Preparation time: 5 minutes

Cooking time: 20 minutes

Servings: 4

Ingredients:

- ¼ cup mozzarella, shredded
- ½ cup coconut cream

- 1 cup white mushrooms
- A pinch of salt and black pepper
- Cooking spray, as needed

Directions:

1. Put the mushrooms in your air fryer's basket, grease with cooking spray, and cook at 370 deg. F for 20 minutes.
2. Transfer to a blender, add the remaining ingredients, pulse well, divide into bowls, and serve as a spread.

Per serving: Calories: 202kcal; Fat: 12g; Carbs: 5g; Protein: 7g

38. Eggs With Dill

Preparation time: 4 minutes

Cooking time: 18 minutes

Servings: 1

Ingredients:

- 2 minced garlic cloves
- 1 tbsp. dill
- 1 tbsp. vinegar
- Salt and pepper to taste
- 1 tbsp. oil
- 1 tbsp. oregano
- 1 tomato (sliced)
- 1 cup olives
- 1 onion (chopped
- 3 eggs

Directions:

1. Whisk eggs in a bowl.
2. Add garlic, dill, vinegar, oregano, tomato, olives, and onion.
3. Grease the round baking tray with oil.
4. Pour the mixture into the baking tray.

5. Let it cook in the air fryer for 18 minutes at 300 deg. F.
6. When ready, serve!

Per serving: Calories: 124kcal; Fat: 7g; Carbs: 10g; Protein: 40g

39. Asparagus Salad

Preparation time: 5 minutes

Cooking time: 10 minutes

Servings: 4

Ingredients:

- 1 cup baby arugula
- 1 bunch asparagus, trimmed
- 1 tbsp. balsamic vinegar
- 1 tbsp. cheddar cheese, grated
- A pinch of salt and black pepper
- Cooking spray, as needed

Directions:

1. Put the asparagus in your air fryer's basket, grease with cooking spray, season with salt and pepper, and cook at 360 deg. F for 10 minutes.
2. Take a bowl and mix the asparagus with the arugula and the vinegar. Toss, divide among plates, and serve hot with cheese sprinkled on top.

Per serving: Calories: 200kcal; Fat: 5g; Carbs: 4g; Protein: 5g

40. Breakfast Fish Tacos

Preparation time: 10 minutes

Cooking time: 13 minutes

Servings: 2

Ingredients:

- 4 large tortillas
- 1 red bell pepper, chopped
- 1 yellow onion, chopped
- 4 white fish fillets, skinless and boneless
- ½ cup salsa
- A handful of mixed romaine lettuce, spinach, and radicchio
- 4 tbsp. Parmesan, grated

Directions:

1. Put the fish fillets in your air fryer and cook them at 350 deg. F for 6 minutes.

2. Meanwhile, heat a pan over medium-high heat, then add the bell pepper and onion. Stir and cook for 1–2 minutes.

3. Arrange the tortillas on a working surface, divide the fish fillets, spread salsa over them, divide the mixed veggies and mixed greens, and spread Parmesan on each at the end.

4. Roll your tacos, place them in the preheated air fryer, and cook them at 350 deg. F for 6 minutes more.

5. Divide the fish tacos among plates, and serve them for breakfast. Enjoy!

Per serving: Calories: 200kcal; Fat: 3g; Carbs: 9g; Protein: 5g

CHAPTER 5: Vegetables

41. Onion Green Beans

Preparation time: 10 minutes

Cooking time: 12 minutes

Servings: 1

Ingredients:

- 11 oz. green beans
- 1 tbsp. onion powder
- 1 tbsp. olive oil
- ½ tsp. salt

Directions:

1. Wash the green beans carefully and place them in the bowl.
2. Sprinkle the green beans with onion powder, salt, and olive oil.
3. Shake the green beans carefully.
4. Preheat the air fryer to 400 deg. F.
5. Put the green beans in the air fryer and cook for 8 minutes.
6. After this, shake the green beans and cook them for 4 minutes more at 400 deg. F.
7. When the time is over, shake the green beans.
8. Serve the side dish and enjoy!

Per serving: Calories: 175kcal; Fat: 7.2g; Carbs: 13.9g; Protein: 63.2g

42. Green Beans And Cherry Tomatoes

Preparation time: 10 minutes

Cooking time: 15 minutes

Servings: 1

Ingredients:

- 8 oz. cherry tomatoes
- 8 oz. green beans
- 1 tbsp. olive oil
- Salt and black pepper, to taste (very little)

Directions:

1. Mix cherry tomatoes with green beans, olive oil, salt, and pepper in a bowl. Mix.
2. Cook in the air fryer at 400 deg. F for 15 minutes. Shake once.
3. Serve.

Per serving: Calories: 162kcal; Fat: 6g; Carbs: 8g; Protein: 8.9g

43. Creamy Cabbage

Preparation time: 10 minutes

Cooking time: 20 minutes

Servings: 1

Ingredients:

- ½ green cabbage head, chopped
- ½ yellow onion, chopped
- Salt and black pepper, to taste (very little)
- ½ cup whipped cream
- 1 tbsp. cornstarch

Directions:

1. Put cabbage and onion in the air fryer.
2. In a bowl, mix cornstarch with cream, salt, and pepper. Stir and pour over cabbage.
3. Mix well and then bake at 400 deg. F for 20 minutes.
4. Serve.

Per serving: Calories: 208kcal; Fat: 10g; Carbs: 16g; Protein: 55g

44. Spiced Almonds

Preparation time: 5 minutes

Cooking time: 12 minutes

Servings: 1

Ingredients:

- ½ tsp. ground cinnamon
- 1 cup almonds
- 1 egg white
- Sea salt to taste (very little)
- Cooking Spray

Directions:

1. Preheat the air fryer to 310 deg. F.
2. Grease the air fryer basket with cooking spray.
3. Take a bowl and split the egg whites of the eggs, being careful of the egg skin chips and removing them if necessary.
4. In a separate bowl, whisk the egg white with cinnamon and the almonds and mix well to flavor the almonds with the egg white and spices.
5. Spread the almonds on the bottom of the frying basket and Air-fry for 12

minutes to 310 deg. F, shaking once or twice. Remove and sprinkle with sea salt to serve.

Per serving: Calories: 90kcal; Fat: 2g; Carbs: 3g; Protein: 45g

45. Mushrooms With Veggies And Avocado

Preparation time: 30 minutes

Cooking time: 8 minutes

Servings: 1

Ingredients:

- 10 ounces mushrooms, halved
- 1 garlic clove, minced
- 1 tablespoon balsamic vinegar
- 1 yellow onion, chopped
- 1 tablespoon olive oil
- Salt and black pepper
- 1 teaspoon basil, dried
- 1 avocado, peeled, pitted, and roughly cubed
- A pinch of red pepper flakes

Directions:

1. Mix the mushrooms with onion, garlic, and avocado in a bowl.
1. Mix the vinegar, oil, salt, pepper, and basil in another bowl and whisk well.
2. Pour this over the vegetables, then toss to coat, set aside for 30 minutes, transfer to the basket of your air fryer, and then cook at 350 degrees F for 8 minutes,
3. Divide between plates and serve with pepper flakes on top as a garnish.

Per serving: Calories: 182kcal; Fat: 3g; Carbs: 5g; Protein: 8g

46. Endives With Seitan Mix

Preparation time: 15 minutes

Cooking time: 10 minutes

Servings: 1

Ingredients:

- 4 endives, trimmed and halved
- Salt and black pepper to taste (very little)
- 1 tbsp. olive oil
- 2 tbsp. seitan, cooked and crumbled
- ½ tsp. nutmeg, ground

Directions:

1. Place the endives in your air fryer's basket, then add the salt and pepper to taste as well as oil and nutmeg; ensure to toss gently.
2. Cook at a temperature of 360 deg. F for 10 minutes.
3. Cut the endives into different plates, sprinkle the seitan as toppings, and serve.

Per serving: Calories: 151kcal; Fat: 6g; Carbs: 14g; Protein: 66g

47. Simple Haddock

Preparation time: 15 minutes

Cooking time: 8 minutes

Servings: 1

Ingredients:

- 2 (6-oz.) vegetarian fillets
- 1 tbsp. olive oil
- Salt and ground black pepper, as required (very little)

Directions:

1. In a bowl, season the fillets with oil, salt, and black pepper.
2. Press the "Power Button" on the Air-fry Oven and turn the dial to select the "Air Fry" mode.
3. Place the fillets in the greased "Air Frying Basket" in the oven.
4. Cook it for 8 minutes at 355 deg. F.
5. Serve.

Per serving: Calories: 151kcal; Fat: 8.6g; Carbs: 0g; Protein: 41.2g

48. Almond Flour Battered And Crisped Onion Rings

Preparation time: 5 minutes

Cooking time: 20 minutes

Servings: 1

Ingredients:

- ½ cup almond flour
- ¾ cup coconut milk
- 1 big white onion, sliced into rings
- 1 egg, beaten
- 1 tbsp. baking powder
- 1 tbsp. paprika, smoked
- Salt and pepper to taste

Directions:

1. Preheat the air fryer oven for 5 minutes.
2. Mix the almond flour, baking powder, smoked paprika, salt, and pepper in a mixing bowl.

3. In another bowl, combine the eggs and coconut milk.
4. Soak the onion slices into the egg mixture.
5. Dredge the onion slices in the almond flour mixture.
6. Pour into the Oven rack/basket. Set temperature to 325 deg. F and set the time to 15 minutes. Select START/STOP to begin. Shake the fryer basket for even cooking.

Per serving: Calories: 217kcal; Fat: 17g; Carbs: 2g; Protein: 5g

49. Herbed Tomatoes

Preparation time: 10 minutes
Cooking time: 15 minutes
Servings: 1
Ingredients:

- 2 big tomatoes, halved and insides scooped out
- Salt and black pepper, to taste (very little)
- ½ tbsp. olive oil
- 1 garlic clove, minced
- ¼ tsp. thyme, chopped

Directions:

1. Mix tomatoes with thyme, garlic, oil, salt, and pepper in the air fryer.
2. Mix and cook at 390 deg. F for 15 minutes.
3. Serve.

Per serving: Calories: 112kcal; Fat: 1g; Carbs: 4g; Protein: 34g

50. Creamy Zucchini And Sweet Potatoes

Preparation time: 10 minutes
Cooking time: 16 minutes
Servings: 1
Ingredients:

- 1 cup veggie stock
- 2 tablespoons olive oil
- 2 sweet potatoes, peeled & cut into medium wedges
- 8 zucchinis, cut into medium wedges
- 2 yellow onions, chopped
- 1 cup coconut milk
- Salt and black pepper to the taste
- 1 tablespoon coconut aminos
- ¼ teaspoon thyme, dried
- ¼ teaspoon rosemary, dried
- 4 tablespoons dill, chopped
- ½ teaspoon basil, chopped

Directions:

1. Heat a skillet that fits your air fryer with the oil over medium heat, add the onion, stir and cook for 2 minutes.
2. Add the zucchini, thyme, rosemary, basil, potato, salt, pepper, broth, milk, amino, and dill, stir, put in your air fryer, cook at 360 degrees F for 14 minutes, divide among plates and serve as a side dish.

Per serving: Calories: 133kcal; Fat: 3g; Carbs: 10g; Protein: 5g

51. Zucchini Squash Mix

Preparation time: 10 minutes
Cooking time: 35 minutes
Servings: 1
Ingredients:

- 1 lb. zucchini, sliced
- 1 tbsp parsley, chopped
- 1 yellow squash, halved, deseeded, and chopped
- 1 tbsp olive oil
- Pepper
- Salt

Directions:

3. Place all ingredients into the large bowl and mix well.
4. Transfer the mixture from the bowl to the air fryer basket and cook at 400 F for 35 minutes.
5. Serve and enjoy.

Per serving: Calories: 49kcal; Fat: 3g; Carbs: 4g; Protein: 1.5g

52. Avocados With Cilantro

Preparation time: 2 minutes
Cooking time: 20 minutes
Servings: 1
Ingredients:

- 2 avocados (diced)
- Salt to taste
- 1 tomato (diced)
- 1 onion (diced)
- 2 jalapeno peppers (chopped)
- ½ tbsp. cilantro (chopped)
- 2 tbsp. lime juice

Directions:

1. Add avocados and onion into the air fryer pot.
2. Mix salt, tomato, jalapeno peppers, cilantro, and lime juice.
3. Cook for 20 minutes at 300 deg. F.
4. When ready, serve and enjoy!

Per serving: Calories: 123kcal; Fat: 2g; Carbs: 10g; Protein: 50g

53. Lemony Baby Potatoes

Preparation time: 10 minutes
Cooking time: 25 minutes
Servings: 1
Ingredients:

- 2 tablespoons olive oil
- 2 springs rosemary, chopped
- 2 tablespoons parsley, chopped
- 2 tablespoons oregano, chopped
- Salt and black pepper to the taste
- 1 tablespoon lemon rind, grated
- 3 garlic cloves, minced
- 2 tablespoons lemon juice
- 2 pounds of baby potatoes

Directions:

1. In a bowl, mix the baby potatoes with the oil, rosemary, parsley, oregano, salt, pepper, lemon zest, garlic, and lemon juice, and transfer the potatoes to the basket of your air fryer and cook at 356 degrees F for 25 minutes.
2. Divide the potatoes between plates and serve as a side dish.

Per serving: Calories: 204kcal; Fat: 4g; Carbs: 17g; Protein: 6g

54. Herbed Tomatoes With Jalapeno

Preparation time: 10 minutes

Cooking time: 8 minutes

Servings: 1

Ingredients:

- 1 jalapeno pepper, chopped
- 4 garlic cloves, minced
- 2 pounds cherry tomatoes, halved
- Salt and black pepper to the taste
- ¼ cup olive oil
- ½ teaspoon oregano, dried
- ¼ cup basil, chopped

Directions:

1. In a huge bowl, toss the tomatoes with the garlic, jalapeño, salt, pepper, oregano, and oil, toss to coat, transfer to your air fryer and cook at 380 degrees F for 15 minutes.
2. Divide the fried tomatoes among the plates, sprinkle the basil on top, and serve as a garnish.

Per serving: Calories: 140kcal; Fat: 2g; Carbs: 6g; Protein: 8g

55. Chard With Cheddar

Preparation time: 10 minutes

Cooking time: 11 minutes

Servings: 1

Ingredients:

- 3 oz. Cheddar cheese, grated
- 10 oz. Swiss chard

- 3 tbsp. creams
- 1 tbsp. sesame oil
- Salt and pepper to taste (very little)

Directions:

1. Wash Swiss chard carefully and chop it roughly.
2. Sprinkle the chopped chard with salt and ground pepper.
3. Stir it carefully.
4. Sprinkle Swiss chard with the sesame oil and stir it carefully with the help of 2 spatulas.
5. Preheat the air fryer to 260 deg. F.
6. Put chopped Swiss chard in the air fryer basket and cook for 6 minutes.
7. Shake it after 3 minutes of cooking.
8. Then pour the cream into the air fryer basket and mix it up.
9. Cook for 3 minutes more.
10. Then increase the temperature to 400 deg. F.
11. Sprinkle with the grated cheese & bake for another 2 minutes.
12. After this, transfer the meal to the serving plates. Enjoy!

Per serving: Calories: 172kcal; Fat: 22.3g; Carbs: 6.7g; Protein: 63.3g

56. Salty Lemon Artichokes

Preparation time: 15 minutes

Cooking time: 45 minutes

Servings: 1

Ingredients:

- 1 lemon
- 2 artichokes
- 1 tsp. kosher salt
- 1 garlic head
- 2 tsp. olive oil

Directions:

1. Cut off the edges of the artichokes.
2. Cut the lemon into halves.
3. Peel the garlic head and chop the garlic cloves roughly.
4. Then place the chopped garlic in the artichokes.
5. Sprinkle the artichokes with olive oil and kosher salt.
6. After that, squeeze the lemon juice into the artichokes.
7. Wrap the artichokes in the foil.
8. Preheat the air fryer to 330 deg. F.
9. Place the wrapped artichokes in the air fryer and cook for 45 minutes.
10. When the artichokes are cooked, discard the foil and serve.
11. Enjoy!

Per serving: Calories: 133kcal; Fat: 5g; Carbs: 21.7g; Protein: 6g

57. Cheesy Roasted Eggplants

Preparation time: 5 minutes

Cooking time: 10-15 minutes

Servings: 1

Ingredients:

- 2 Eggplants, sliced
- 1 tsp. sesame oil
- Sea salt & freshly ground black pepper, to taste (very little)
- ½ tsp. parsley flakes
- 1 tsp. garlic, pressed
- ½ cup cream cheese, at room temperature

Directions:

1. Brush your eggplants with sesame oil; season them with salt and black pepper, and place them in the Air Fryer cooking basket.
2. Cook your eggplants at 400 deg. F for 10 minutes.
3. And then, mix the remaining ingredients to make the rub. Top the eggplant with the resulting mixture and continue cooking for another 5 minutes.
4. Place your eggplants on a serving platter. Serve and enjoy.

Per serving: Calories: 185kcal; Fat: 19.8g; Carbs: 16g; Protein: 56.6g

58. Veg Buffalo Cauliflower

Preparation time: 20 minutes

Cooking time: 15 minutes

Servings: 1

Ingredients:

- 1 medium head cauliflower
- 1 tsp. avocado oil
- 1 tbsp. red hot sauce
- 1 tbsp. nutritional yeast
- 1 ½ tsp. maple syrup
- ¼ tsp. sea salt
- 1 tbsp. cornstarch or arrowroot starch

Directions:

1. Set your air fryer toaster oven to 360 deg. F. Place all the ingredients into a bowl except cauliflower. Mix them to combine.
2. Put the cauliflower and mix to coat equally. Put half of your cauliflower into an air fryer and cook for 15 minutes but keep shaking them until you get desired consistency.
3. Do the same for the cauliflower, which is left, except lower the cooking time to 10 minutes.
4. Keep the cauliflower tightly sealed in the refrigerator for 3-4 days. For heating again, add back to the air fryer for 1-2 minutes until crispness.

Per serving: Calories: 248kcal; Fat: 20g; Carbs: 13g; Protein: 4g

59. Flatbread

Preparation time: 5 minutes

Cooking time: 7 minutes

Servings: 1

Ingredients:

- 1 cup mozzarella cheese, shredded
- ¼ cup almond flour
- 1 oz. full-fat cream cheese softened

Directions:

1. Melt mozzarella in the microwave for 30 seconds. Stir in almond flour until smooth.
2. Add cream cheese. Continue mixing until dough forms. Knead with wet hands if necessary.
3. Divide the dough into two pieces and then roll out to ¼-inch thickness between 2 pieces of parchment.
4. Cover the air fryer basket with parchment and place the flatbreads into the air fryer basket. Work in batches if necessary.
5. Cook at 320 deg. F for 7 minutes. Flip once at the halfway mark.
6. Serve.

Per serving: Calories: 296kcal; Fat: 22.6g; Carbs: 3.3g; Protein: 16.3g

60. Soft Tofu With Veggies

Preparation time: 10 minutes

Cooking time: 14 minutes

Servings: 1

Ingredients:

- 1 tomato, chopped
- 3 carrots, chopped and steamed
- 2 ounces soft tofu, crumbled
- 1 teaspoon parsley, chopped
- 1 teaspoon thyme, chopped
- Salt and black pepper to the taste

Directions:

1. In a skillet that fits your air fryer, combine tomato, carrots, thyme, parsley, salt, and pepper, toss, insert fryer and cook at 350 degrees F for 10 minutes.
2. Add the tofu, mix, put in the air fryer for four more minutes, divide between plates and serve as a side dish.

Per serving: Calories: 174kcal; Fat: 4g; Carbs: 12g; Protein: 3g

CHAPTER 6: Snacks

61. Delicious Mushroom Mix Side Dish

Preparation time: 4 minutes

Cooking time: 20 minutes

Servings: 1

Ingredients:

- ¼ cup oil
- ¼ cup flour (all-purpose)
- 1 bell pepper
- 1 onion (chopped)
- 2 cups chicken (chopped breast)
- 4.5 oz. mushrooms
- 4.5 oz. tomatoes – diced
- 2 tsp. sauce (any)
- 3 garlic cloves
- 1 tsp. soy sauce
- 1 tsp. sugar (white)
- Salt and pepper to taste
- 3 drops of hot sauce

Directions:

1. Grease the baking tray with oil.
2. Add flour and chicken into a bowl.
3. Mix bell pepper, onion, mushrooms, tomatoes, sauce, garlic cloves, soy sauce, sugar, and hot sauce with salt and pepper.
4. Pour the mixture into the baking tray.
5. Cook in the air fryer for 20 minutes at 300 deg. F.
6. When ready, serve!

Per serving: Calories: 70kcal; Fat: 6g; Carbs: 10g; Protein: 10g

62. Avocados With Tomatillos

Preparation time: 2 minutes

Cooking time: 10 minutes

Servings: 1

Ingredients:

- 3 avocados (peeled)
- 3 tomatillos (chopped)
- 1 red onion (chopped)
- 2 tomatoes (chopped)
- 1 tbsp. lime juice
- 1 tbsp. red pepper flakes
- 2 drops of hot pepper sauce
- Salt and pepper to taste

Directions:

1. Add avocados and tomatillos into a bowl.
2. Mix red onion, tomatoes, lime juice, red pepper flakes, and hot pepper.
3. Pour the mixture into the air fryer pot.
4. Cook for 10 minutes at 300 deg. F.
5. When ready, sprinkle salt and pepper to serve!

Per serving: Calories: 105kcal; Fat: 9g; Carbs: 10g; Protein: 30g

63. Whole Wheat Air Fried Pizzas

Preparation time: 5 minutes

Cooking time: 4/5 minutes

Servings: 1

Ingredients:

- ¼ cup lower-sodium marinara sauce
- 2 whole-wheat pita rounds
- 1 cup baby spinach leaves
- 1 small plum tomato
- 1 small garlic clove
- ¼ cup pre-shredded part-skim mozzarella cheese
- 1 tbsp. shaved Parmigiano-Reggiano cheese

Directions:

1. Warm the Air Fryer to 350 deg. F.
2. Spread the marinara sauce over one side of each pita bread.
3. Slice the tomato into eight slices and thinly slice the garlic.
4. Top each one-off using half of the spinach leaves, tomato slices, garlic, and cheeses.
5. Place one pita in the fryer basket, and air-fry to 350 deg. F until the cheese is melted and the pita is crispy (4-5 minutes).
6. Repeat with the remaining pita and serve.

Per serving: Calories: 149kcal; Fat: 5g; Carbs: 37g; Protein: 61g

64. Pumpkin Quick Dish

Preparation time: 3 minutes

Cooking time: 12 minutes

Servings: 1

Ingredients:

- ¼ pumpkin (peeled, sliced)
- 1 ginger (cut)
- 2 tbsp. soy sauce
- 3 oz. Tofu (cubed)
- 2 green onions (chopped)
- 2 red peppers (sliced)
- 2 tbsp. sesame seeds
- 2 tbsp. cilantro (chopped)
- 2 tbsp. ginger pickles

Directions:

1. Add pumpkin and ginger into the air fryer pot.
2. Cook for 2 minutes at 300 deg. F.
3. Mix soy sauce, tofu, green onion, red peppers, sesame seeds, and ginger pickles.
4. Cook for another 10 minutes.
5. When ready, garnish cilantro and serve!

Per serving: Calories: 115kcal; Fat: 7g; Carbs: 9g; Protein: 40g

65. Kale Chips

Preparation time: 5 minutes
Cooking time: 7 minutes
Servings: 1
Ingredients:

- 1 bunch of curly kale
- 2 tsp. olive oil
- 1 tbsp. nutritional yeast
- ⅛ tsp. black pepper
- ¼ tsp. sea salt

Directions:

1. Warm the Air Fryer unit to reach 390 deg. F.
2. Thoroughly rinse the kale and pat it dry. Remove the leaves from the stems of the kale and toss them into a mixing container.
3. Add the olive oil, salt, pepper, and nutritional yeast. Use your hands to massage the toppings into the kale leaves.
4. Scoop the kale into the fryer basket and air-fry them until they are crispy (6-7 minutes).
5. Note: If using a small Air Fryer, cook the chips in two batches. You don't want to overfill the fryer basket.
6. Enjoy them piping hot or slightly cooled.
7. Save any leftover chips in a zip-top bag for up to five days.

Per serving: Calories: 90kcal; Fat: 5.3g; Carbs: 9.1g; Protein: 33.8g

66. Navy Beans With Molasses

Preparation time: 4 minutes
Cooking time: 10 minutes
Servings: 1
Ingredients:

- 1 lb. dried navy beans
- 2 cups water
- Salt to taste
- 10 oz. bacon (slices)
- 1 onion (chopped)
- 1 cup molasses
- 1 tbsp. ketchup
- 1 tbsp. brown sugar
- 1 tbsp. dry mustard
- Pepper to taste

Directions:

1. Add navy beans and water into the air fryer pot.
2. Cook for 10 minutes at 300 deg. F.
3. Mix bacon, onion, molasses, ketchup, brown sugar, dry mustard, and pepper.
4. Cook for another 14 minutes.
5. When ready, serve and enjoy!

Per serving: Calories: 70kcal; Fat: 6g; Carbs: 10g; Protein: 10g

67. Avocado Jalapeno Side Dish

Preparation time: 3 minutes
Cooking time: 15 minutes
Servings: 1
Ingredients:

- 4 avocados (peeled)
- 2 tbsp. lime juice

- 2 tbsp. lemon juice
- 2 cans of tomatoes (diced)
- ½ cup red onion (diced)
- 1 large jalapeno pepper (minced)
- 3 cloves garlic (minced)
- Salt and pepper to taste

Directions:

1. Mash avocados into the bowl.
2. Mix lime juice, lemon juice, tomatoes, red onions, jalapeno pepper, and garlic with salt and pepper.
3. Pour the mixture into the air fryer and cook for 15 minutes on high pressure.
4. When done, serve and enjoy!

Per serving: Calories: 91kcal; Fat: 4g; Carbs: 10g; Protein: 25.7g

68. Onion Mix Tofu Side Dish

Preparation time: 2 minutes
Cooking time: 20 minutes
Servings: 1
Ingredients:

- 2 tbsp. oil
- 1 onion (chopped)
- 2 cloves garlic (chopped)
- 2 cups tofu
- 1 tbsp. soy sauce
- 1 carrot (grated)
- Salt and pepper to taste
- 2 cups spinach (chopped)

Directions:

1. Add oil and onion into the air fryer pot.
2. Cook for 10 minutes at 300 deg. F.
3. Mix garlic, tofu, soy sauce, carrots, salt, and pepper with spinach.
4. Cook for another 10 minutes.
5. When ready, serve!

Per serving: Calories: 70kcal; Fat: 6g; Carbs: 10g; Protein: 10g

69. Kale Mix Snack

Preparation time: 3 minutes
Cooking time: 10 minutes
Servings: 1
Ingredients:

- 2 cups Kale
- 2 tbsp. oil
- Salt to taste
- 1 tbsp. lemon zest
- 1 cup almonds (chopped)

Directions:

1. Add oil into the air fryer pot.
2. Mix kale, salt, lemon zest, and almonds.
3. Cook at 300 deg. F for 10 minutes.
4. When ready, serve and enjoy!

Per serving: Calories: 86kcal; Fat: 6g; Carbs: 10g; Protein: 20.1g

70. Sweet Potato Tots

Preparation time: 10 minutes
Cooking time: 31 minutes
Servings: 24
Ingredients:

- 2 sweet potatoes, peeled
- 1/2 tsp. Cajun seasoning
- Salt, to taste
- 1 cup Water

- Cooking spray, as needed

Directions:

1. Pour the water into a pot, boil it, and add the sweet potatoes. Boil for 15 minutes, then drains well.
2. Grate the boiled sweet potatoes into a bowl.
3. Put the Cajun seasoning plus salt in the grated sweet potatoes, and mix until well combined.
4. Lightly spray your air fryer basket using a cooking spray.
5. Form a small tot of the mixture and put it in an air fryer basket.
6. Cook at 400 deg. F for 8 minutes. Turn the sweet potato tots to another side and cook them for 8 minutes more. Serve and enjoy.

Per serving: Calories: 15kcal; Fat: 0g; Carbs: 3.5g; Protein: 0.2g

CHAPTER 7: Dressings, Sauces, And Seasonings

71. Romesco Sauce

Preparation time: 5 minutes

Cooking time: 15 minutes

Servings: 10

Ingredients:

- 1/2 tsp of salt
- 2 garlic cloves
- 1/2 cup of olive oil
- 1 tsp of sweet paprika
- 1/4 tsp of ground pepper
- 1/2 cup of roasted tomatoes
- 2 tbsp of fresh parsley, minced
- 1/2 cup of almonds, toasted
- 1 jar of sweet red peppers, roasted
- 1/2 cup of whole wheat crumbs

Directions:

1. Add everything to the air fryer basket and cook for about 15 minutes at 350 degrees F.
2. Let it cool, and then store it in a jar.

Per serving: Calories: 155kcal; Fat: 10g; Carbs: 23g; Protein: 5g

72. Carrot Sauce

Preparation time: 20 minutes

Cooking time: 20 minutes

Servings: 10

Ingredients:

- 1 tbsp of salt
- 1 tsp of black pepper
- 2 tbsp of olive oil
- 1 red onion, diced
- 2 tbsp of chili powder
- 4 cloves of garlic, minced
- 6 ripe tomatoes, chopped
- 1 tbsp of balsamic vinegar
- 1 cup of white wine
- 1 tsp of Italian seasoning
- 1 cup of carrots, chopped

Directions:

1. Mix all the ingredients in a bowl, then add to the air fryer basket.
2. Cook for about 20 minutes at 530 deg. F.
3. Have it with your favorite pasta.

Per serving: Calories: 90kcal; Fat: 8g; Carbs: 2g; Protein: 2g

73. Cranberry Sauce

Preparation time: 5 minutes

Cooking time: 25 minutes

Servings: 2

Ingredients:

- 1/2 cup of water
- 1/8 tsp of salt
- 1/8 tsp of ground cloves
- 1 3/4 cups of brown sugar
- 1/8 tsp of ground ginger
- 1/2 tsp of ground allspice
- 1 pack of frozen cranberries
- 1/2 tsp of ground cinnamon

Directions:

1. Combine all the ingredients in a bowl. Transfer into air fryer basket.
2. Cook in the air fryer at 400 deg. F for about 20 minutes. Let it cool, and store it in the refrigerator.

Per serving: Calories: 135kcal; Fat: 5g; Carbs: 20g; Protein: 3g

74. Dumpling Sauce

Preparation time: 5 minutes
Cooking time: 5 minutes
Servings: 3
Ingredients:

- 1 tbsp of water
- 1 tbsp of soy sauce
- 1 tbsp of rice vinegar
- 1 tsp of sesame oil
- 1/2 tsp of sesame seeds
- 1 tbsp of brown sugar
- Chopped scallions

Directions:

1. Mix all the ingredients and add them to the air fryer basket.
2. Cook for about 5 minutes at 350 deg. F. Enjoy with dumplings.

Per serving: Calories: 70kcal; Fat: 5g; Carbs: 5g; Protein: 5g

75. Chives Soy Sauce

Preparation time: 5 minutes
Cooking time: 5 minutes
Servings: 5
Ingredients:

- 1 bunch of dallae

- Pinch of salt
- Pinch of sesame seeds
- 3 tbsp of soy sauce
- 2 tbsp of honey

Directions:

1. Mix all the ingredients in a bowl, then add them to the air fryer basket.
2. Cook for about 5 minutes at 320 deg. F. Enjoy.

Per serving: Calories: 120kcal; Fat: 0.9g; Carbs: 1.4g; Protein: 2g

76. BBQ Sauce

Preparation time: 5 minutes
Cooking time: 5 minutes
Servings: 4
Ingredients:

- 1 tbsp of cornstarch
- 1 cup of soy sauce
- 3/4 cup of brown sugar
- 1 tsp of sesame oil
- 2 tbsp of minced garlic
- 1 tbsp of garlic sauce
- 1 tsp of grated fresh ginger
- 1 tbsp of rice vinegar
- 1 1/2 tsp of ground black pepper

Directions:

1. Add everything to the air fryer basket and cook for about 15 minutes at 400 deg. F.
2. Let it cool. Serve and enjoy!

Per serving: Calories: 219kcal; Fat: 1.3g; Carbs: 50g; Protein: 5g

77. Dipping Sauce

Preparation time: 3 minutes
Cooking time: 5 minutes
Servings: 8
Ingredients:

- 4 tbsp of water
- 1/4 cup of soy sauce
- 2 red chili pepper, crushed
- 1 tbsp of rice vinegar
- 3 tbsp of sliced green onions
- 1 1/2 tbsp of brown sugar
- 1 1/2 tsp of sesame seeds, roasted

Directions:

1. Combine all the ingredients and pour them into the air fryer basket.
2. Cook for about 5 minutes at 300 deg. F. Serve and enjoy!

Per serving: Calories: 12kcal; Fat: 0.3g; Carbs: 1.7g; Protein: 0.6g

78. Fried Chicken Sauce

Preparation time: 5 minutes
Cooking time: 5 minutes
Servings: 4
Ingredients:

- 1 tbsp of gochujang paste
- 1 tbsp of honey
- 2 tbsp of rice vinegar
- 5 tbsp of water
- 3 tbsp of tomato ketchup

Directions:

1. Combine all the ingredients and pour them into the air fryer basket.
2. Cook for about 5 minutes at 300 deg. F. Serve and enjoy.

Per serving: Calories: 120kcal; Fat: 0.5g; Carbs: 12g; Protein: 1.2g

79. Vegan Mayo Sauce

Preparation time: 15 minutes
Cooking time: 2 minutes
Servings: 10
Ingredients:

- 1/2 cup of aquafaba
- 1 tsp of maple syrup
- 1 1/2 tsp of black pepper
- 2 tsp of chili powder
- 1/2 tsp of sea salt
- 1/2 cup of chili oil

Directions:

1. Mix all the ingredients in a bowl and add to the air fryer basket.
2. Cook for about 5 minutes at 350 deg. F.
3. Store it in an air-tight container.

Per serving: Calories: 82kcal; Fat: 9g; Carbs: 1g; Protein: 1g

80. Sesame Sauce

Preparation time: 5 minutes
Cooking time: 5 minutes
Servings: 4
Ingredients:

- 4 tbsp of soy sauce
- 1/2 tsp of brown sugar
- 2 tbsp of sesame oil
- 2 tbsp of rice vinegar
- 1 tsp of roasted sesame seeds

- 1 finely chopped scallion

Directions:

1. Mix all the ingredients and add them to the air fryer basket.

2. Cook for about 5 minutes at 300 deg. F. Enjoy.

Per serving: Calories: 20kcal; Fat: 0.9g; Carbs: 10g; Protein: 2g

CHAPTER 8: Poultry And Meat Recipes

81. Air Fried Chicken Fillets

Preparation time: 10 minutes

Cooking time: 15 minutes

Servings: 3

Ingredients:

- 2 eggs
- 2 tbsp of vegetable oil
- 12 ounces of chicken fillets
- 1/2 teaspoon salt
- 1 tsp of black pepper
- 8 tbsp of breadcrumbs
- 4 ounces of almond flour

Directions:

1. Preheat the air fryer to 330 degrees F.
2. Mix oil, pepper, and salt in breadcrumbs and mix well.
3. Add chicken fillets into flour and then into the egg mixture.
4. Then coat with breadcrumb mixture.
5. Put these into sprayed air fryer basket.
6. Cook for about 15 minutes at 390 deg. F.
7. Serve and enjoy.

Per serving: Calories: 162kcal; Fat: 4g; Carbs: 0g; Protein: 30g

82. Garlic Chicken Wings

Preparation time: 8 minutes

Cooking time: 30 minutes

Servings: 6

Ingredients:

- 1 tsp of salt
- 2 lb of chicken wings
- 1 tsp of parsley
- 2 tbsp of minced garlic
- 1/4 tsp of pepper
- 3/4 cup of Parmesan cheese, grated

Directions:

1. Mix all ingredients in a bowl. Mix wings in it.
2. Cook wings in the air fryer for about 28 minutes at 400 deg. F.
3. Flip and cook for about 12 minutes. Serve with ketchup and enjoy.

Per serving: Calories: 350kcal; Fat: 23g; Carbs: 11g; Protein: 37g

83. Chicken Drumettes

Preparation time: 15 minutes

Cooking time: 15 minutes

Servings: 3

Ingredients:

- 3/4 tsp of brown sugar
- 1 tsp of sesame oil
- 3 tsp of prawn paste
- 1 tsp of ginger juice
- 1/2 tsp of Shaoxing wine
- 1/2 ounces of chicken drumettes
- 6 tsp of vegetable oil

Directions:

1. Mix the brown sugar, sesame oil, wine, ginger juice, and prawn paste to form the marinade.

2. Marinate chicken overnight in the fridge.
3. Preheat the air fryer for about 5 minutes at 356 deg. F.
4. Spray chicken with vegetable oil and place in an air fryer basket.
5. Cook for about 7 minutes, turn the drumettes over and cook for another 8 minutes until golden.
6. Serve and enjoy.

Per serving: Calories: 90kcal; Fat: 7g; Carbs: 3g; Protein: 5g

84. Chicken With Citrus Sauce

Preparation time: 10 minutes
Cooking time: 12 minutes
Servings: 4
Ingredients:

- 2 tbsp of water
- 1 orange zest
- 2 tsp of cornstarch
- 1 tsp of soy sauce
- 2 tbsp of cornstarch
- 1/2 cup of orange juice
- 2 tbsp of brown sugar
- 1 tsp of rice wine vinegar
- 1 tsp of ground ginger
- Red pepper flakes
- 1 pound of boneless chicken breasts

Directions:

1. Preheat the air fryer to 400 deg. F.
2. Coat chicken with cornstarch.
3. Cook for 9 minutes in the air fryer.

4. Mix and cook all the other ingredients in a pan to make the sauce.
5. Add cornstarch and water to it and cook for about five more minutes.
6. Serve chicken with sauce and enjoy.

Per serving: Calories: 630kcal; Fat: 15g; Carbs: 46g; Protein: 75g

85. Healthy Sausage Mix

Preparation time: 10 minutes
Cooking time: 10 minutes
Servings: 4
Ingredients:

- 2 tbsp of mustard
- 1 bell pepper. diced
- 1/3 cup of ketchup
- 1/2 cup of chicken stock
- 3 tbsp of brown sugar
- 1/2 cup of chopped onion
- 1 pound of sliced sausages
- 2 tbsp of apple cider vinegar

Directions:

1. Mix all the ingredients in a bowl.
2. Pour into the pan of the air fryer and cook for about 10 minutes at 350 deg. F.
3. Serve and enjoy.

Per serving: Calories: 162kcal; Fat: 6g; Carbs: 12g; Protein: 6g

86. Steak With Cabbage

Preparation time: 10 minutes
Cooking time: 10 minutes
Servings: 4
Ingredients:

- 2 tsp of cornstarch
- 1 tbsp of peanut oil
- 1 chopped yellow bell pepper
- 2 chopped green onions
- 2 minced garlic cloves
- Salt & black pepper, as per taste
- 2 cups of chopped green cabbage
- 1/2 pound of sirloin steak, diced

Directions:

1. Mix cabbage, peanut oil, black pepper, and salt in a bowl.
2. Place in the basket and cook for around 5 minutes at 370 deg. F.
3. Add steak to the air fryer and mix the rest of the ingredients.
4. Cook for around 5 minutes.
5. Serve with cabbage.

Per serving: Calories: 282kcal; Fat: 6g; Carbs: 14g; Protein: 6g

87. Healthy Chicken Casserole

Preparation time: 20 minutes
Cooking time: 17 minutes
Servings: 6
Ingredients:

- 1 cup of salsa
- Cooking spray
- 2 tsp of chili powder
- 2 tsp of ground cumin
- 1 tbsp of garlic powder
- 6 chopped kale leaves
- 1 cup of tomato sauce
- 1/2 cup of chopped cilantro
- 1 cup of quinoa, cooked
- 2 chopped jalapeno peppers
- 1/2 cup of chopped green onions
- 12 ounces of black beans, canned
- 3 cups of mozzarella cheese, grated
- 3 cups of boiled chicken breast, shredded

Directions:

1. Spray the dish with cooking spray and all ingredients in it. Mix well. Cook in the air fryer for about 17 minutes at 350 deg. F.
2. Serve and enjoy.

Per serving: Calories: 365kcal; Fat: 12g; Carbs: 22g; Protein: 26g

88. Cornish Chicken

Preparation time: 10 minutes
Cooking time: 25 minutes
Servings: 2
Ingredients:

- Salt
- Olive oil
- 1 lemon
- 1 Cornish chicken
- Black pepper

Directions:

1. Preheat the air fryer at390 deg. F. Coat, the chicken with olive oil.
2. Squeeze lemon inside it. Add any stuffing if you want.
3. Season it well with salt and pepper. Tie it with a string.
4. Spray the air fryer basket with olive oil.
5. Cook chicken for about 25 minutes until golden brown.
6. Serve and enjoy.

Per serving: Calories: 566kcal; Fat: 45g; Carbs: 0g; Protein: 50g

89. Salami Bites

Preparation time: 5 minutes

Cooking time: 5 minutes

Servings: 10

Ingredients:

- Filling
- Olive oil
- Spices
- 10 pieces of salami

Directions:

1. Place salami pieces on each other in the ramekin.
2. Cook in the air fryer for about 4 minutes at 400 deg. F.
3. Let it cool, and then add filling to it. Enjoy.

Per serving: Calories: 217kcal; Fat: 14g; Carbs: 15g; Protein: 7g

90. Herbal Chicken And Sweet Potatoes

Preparation time: 5 minutes

Cooking time: 23 minutes

Servings: 2

Ingredients:

- 1 sweet potato
- 1 tsp of olive oil
- Salad greens
- 1/2 portion of chicken, halved
- 1 tbsp of herbs, chicken spices

Directions:

1. Marinate chicken with olive oil and herb spices for an hour in the fridge.
2. Cook sweet potato in the air fryer for about 10 minutes at 350 deg. F.
3. Then cook marinated chicken pieces in the air fryer for 12 minutes until golden brown.
4. Serve with salad greens and enjoy.

Per serving: Calories: 220kcal; Fat: 7g; Carbs: 18g; Protein: 16g

91. Korean Beef

Preparation time: 20 minutes

Cooking time: 30 minutes

Servings: 6

Ingredients:

- Coconut oil spray
- 1 lb of flank steak
- 1/2 cup of brown sugar
- 1/4 cup of cornstarch
- 1 tsp of ground ginger
- 1/2 cup of soy sauce, gluten-free

- 1 tbsp of chili sauce
- 2 tbsp of white wine vinegar
- 1 clove of garlic, minced
- 1/2 tsp of sesame seeds
- 1 tbsp of water

Directions:

1. Mix steak pieces and cornstarch. Line the air fryer basket with foil.
2. Cook steak pieces for about 20 minutes at 390 deg. F.
3. Add all the other ingredients to a pan to make the sauce.
4. Pour this sauce over the meat, then serve with rice or beans.

Per serving: Calories: 489kcal; Fat: 22g; Carbs: 32g; Protein: 38g

92. Cheesy Scotch Eggs

Preparation time: 5 minutes

Cooking time: 12 minutes

Servings: 2

Ingredients:

- 6 eggs
- 3/4 lbs of sausage
- 1/4 cup of parmesan cheese, shredded

Directions:

1. Preheat the air fryer to 390 deg. F. Boil eggs.
2. Peel eggs and set them aside.
3. Divide sausage into equal portions.
4. Roll sausages with a wrap; it should look like a small pancake.
5. Wrap the egg in it. Do the same with all eggs.

6. Coat the outer surface with cheese.
7. Put these in an air fryer basket and cook for about 12 minutes. Serve and enjoy.

Per serving: Calories: 233kcal; Fat: 25g; Carbs: 23g; Protein: 20g

93. Chicken Kebabs

Preparation time: 10 minutes

Cooking time: 20 minutes

Servings: 2

Ingredients:

- 1/4 cup of honey
- Cooking spray
- 1/3 cup of soy sauce
- 6 mushrooms, chopped
- 3 bell peppers, diced
- 2 chicken breasts, chopped
- Salt & black pepper, as per taste

Directions:

1. Combine the chicken, salt, honey, pepper, soy sauce, and oil in a large mixing bowl.
2. Mash everything together with mushrooms and bell peppers.
3. Make kebabs and air fry for about 20 minutes at 338 deg. F. Serve and enjoy.

Per serving: Calories: 261kcal; Fat: 7g; Carbs: 12g; Protein: 6g

94. Turkey Breast

Preparation time: 2 hours

Cooking time: 1 hour

Servings: 8

Ingredients:

- 2 tsp of olive oil
- 1 turkey breast
- 1/2 cup of cooking oil
- 1/2 tsp of kosher salt
- 1/2 tsp o black pepper
- 1/2 tsp of garlic
- 1/2 tsp of onion
- 1 tsp of powder dark chili
- For Brine
- 1 carrot
- 1/2 gallon of cold water
- 1/4 cup of kosher salt
- 1/4 cup of brown sugar
- 3 cloves garlic, halved
- 1 tbsp of black peppercorns
- 1 quartered yellow onion
- 1/4 bunch of fresh parsley
- A few bay leaves

Directions:

1. Boil water in a pot. Mix brown sugar and salt in it.
2. Take off the flame and mix the rest of the ingredients in it.
3. Allow it to cool. Put turkey in the mixture and place in the fridge for around 2 hours.
4. Rub oil after drying the breast.
5. Season using spices and salt. Warm half a cup of cooking oil in a pan.
6. Cook turkey in the air fryer for around 50 minutes at 400 deg. F.
7. Serve and enjoy.

Per serving: Calories: 160kcal; Fat: 4g; Carbs: 9g; Protein: 21g

95. Herb Flavored Lamb

Preparation time: 10 minutes

Cooking time: 10 minutes

Servings: 4

Ingredients:

- salt
- 1 rack of lamb
- pepper
- 2 tbsp of dried rosemary
- 1 tbsp of dried thyme
- 4 tbsp of olive oil
- 2 tsp of minced garlic

Directions:

1. Mix herbs in a bowl along with oil.
2. Mix and coat lamb with it.
3. Place in the air fryer and cook for around 10 minutes at 360 deg. F.
4. Serve and enjoy.

Per serving: Calories: 346kcal; Fat: 11g; Carbs: 23g; Protein: 34g

CHAPTER 9: Seafood Recipes

96. Caramelized Salmon Fillet

Preparation time: 5 minutes

Cooking time: 25 minutes

Servings: 4

Ingredients:

- 2 salmon fillets
- 60g cane sugar
- 4 tbsp soy sauce
- 50g sesame seeds
- Unlimited Ginger

Directions:

1. Preheat the air fryer to 180oC for 5 minutes.
2. Put the sugar and soy sauce in the basket.
3. Cook everything for 5 minutes.
4. In the meantime, wash the fish, pass it through sesame to cover it completely, place it inside the tank, and add the fresh ginger.
5. Cook for 12 minutes.
6. Turn the fish over and finish cooking for another 8 minutes.

Per serving: Calories: 569kcal; Fat: 14.9g; Carbs: 40g; Protein: 66.9g

97. Salted Marinated Salmon

Preparation time: 10 minutes

Cooking time: 30 minutes

Servings: 4

Ingredients:

- 500g salmon fillet
- 1 kg coarse salt

Directions:

1. Place the baking paper on the air fryer basket and the salmon on top (skin side up) covered with coarse salt.
2. Set the air fryer to 1500C.
3. Cook everything for 25 to 30 minutes. At the end of cooking, remove the salt from the fish and serve with a drizzle of oil.

Per serving: Calories: 290kcal; Fat: 13g; Carbs: 3gg; Protein: 40g

98. Salmon With Pistachio Bark

Preparation time: 10 minutes

Cooking time: 30 minutes

Servings: 4

Ingredients:

- 600 g salmon fillet
- 50g pistachios
- Salt to taste

Directions:

1. Put the parchment paper on the bottom of the air fryer basket and place the salmon fillet in it (it can be cooked whole or already divided into four portions).
2. Cut the pistachios into thick pieces; grease the top of the fish and salt (little because the pistachios are already salted), and cover everything with the pistachios.

3. Set the air fryer to 1800C and simmer for 25 minutes.

Per serving: Calories: 371.7kcal; Fat: 21.8g; Carbs: 9.4g; Protein: 34.7g

99. Noodles And Tuna Fish

Preparation time: 4 minutes

Cooking time: 15 minutes

Servings: 1

Ingredients:

- 1 lb. tuna fish
- 1 small pack of noodles
- 1 lb. Bok choy
- Salt to taste
- 4 cups chicken stock
- 2 cups hot water

Directions:

1. Add the chicken stock into the air fryer pot.
2. Mix the pot with tuna fish, Bok choy, noodles, salt, and hot water.
3. Cook at 300 deg. F for 10 minutes.
4. When ready, serve and enjoy!

Per serving: Calories: 155kcal; Fat: 7g; Carbs: 10g; Protein: 40g

100. Cod Fish Nuggets

Preparation time: 5 minutes

Cooking time: 20 minutes

Servings: 4

Ingredients:

- Cod fillet (1 lb.)
- Eggs (3)
- Olive oil (4 tbsp.)
- Almond flour (1 cup)
- Gluten-free breadcrumbs (1 cup)

Directions:

1. Warm the Air Fryer to 390º Fahrenheit.
2. Slice the cod into nuggets.
3. Prepare three bowls. Whisk the eggs in one. Combine the salt, oil, and breadcrumbs in another. Sift the almond flour into the third one.
4. Cover each nugget with flour, and dip in the eggs and the breadcrumbs.
5. Arrange the nuggets in the basket and set the timer for 20 minutes.
6. Serve the fish with your favorite dips or sides.

Per serving: Calories: 334kcal; Fat: 10g; Carbs: 8g; Protein: 32g

101. Shrimp, Zucchini And Cherry Tomato Sauce

Preparation time: 5 minutes

Cooking time: 30 minutes

Servings: 4

Ingredients:

- 2 zucchinis
- 300 shrimp
- 7 cherry tomatoes
- Salt and pepper to taste
- 1 clove garlic

Directions:

1. Pour the oil into the air fryer, and add the garlic clove and diced zucchini.
2. Cook for 15 minutes at 1500C.

3. Add the shrimp and the pieces of tomato, salt, and spices.

4. Cook for another 5 to 10 minutes or until the shrimp water evaporates.

Per serving: Calories: 214.3kcal; Fat: 8.6g; Carbs: 7.8g; Protein: 27.0g

102. Spinach With Salmon And Seashells

Preparation time: 5 minutes
Cooking time: 10 minutes
Servings: 1
Ingredients:

- 1 lb. seashells
- 1 pack spinach (chopped)
- 2 tbsp. oil
- 7 cloves garlic (minced)
- 1 lb. salmon (chopped)
- 1 tsp. red pepper flakes
- Salt for taste

Directions:

1. Add oil into the air fryer pot.
2. Mix salt with tuna fish, garlic, red pepper flakes, spinach, and seashells.
3. Cook at 300 deg. F for 15 minutes.
4. When the pot beeps, serve and enjoy!

Per serving: Calories: 100 kcal; Fat: 10g; Carbs: 8g; Protein: 11.5g

103. Grilled Sardines

Preparation time: 5 minutes
Cooking time: 20 minutes
Servings: 4
Ingredients:

- 5 sardines
- Herbs of Provence

Directions:

1. Preheat the air fryer to 1600C.
2. Spray the basket and place your sardines in the basket of your fryer.
3. Set the timer for 14 minutes. After 7 minutes, remember to turn the sardines so that they are roasted on both sides.

Per serving: Calories: 189kcal; Fat: 10g; Carbs: 10g; Protein: 22g

104. Cabbage With Salmon Fish

Preparation time: 6 minutes
Cooking time: 15 minutes
Servings: 1
Ingredients:

- ½ tsp. sesame oil
- 1 tbsp. canola oil
- 2 tbsp. Chile paste
- 2 cloves garlic (chopped)
- 4 Salmon fish (cubes)
- ½ cup soy sauce
- 1 onion (sliced)
- ½ cabbage (chopped)
- 2 carrots (chopped)
- 8 oz. noodles (cooked)

Directions:

1. Add sesame oil and canola oil into the air fryer pot.
2. Mix garlic and salmon cubes.
3. Add onion, soy sauce, Chile paste, cabbage, and carrots.
4. Cook at 300 deg. F for 15 minutes.

5. When ready, serve with noodles.

Per serving: Calories: 90kcal; Fat: 8g; Carbs: 20g; Protein: 25g

105. Creamy Salmon

Preparation time: 5 minutes

Cooking time: 20 minutes

Servings: 4

Ingredients:

- Chopped dill (1 tbsp.)
- Olive oil (1 tbsp.)
- Sour cream (3 tbsp.)
- Plain yogurt (1.76 oz.)
- Salmon (6 pieces)/.75 lb.)

Directions:

1. Heat the Air Fryer and wait for it to reach 285⁰ Fahrenheit.
2. Shake the salt over the salmon and add them to the fryer basket with the olive oil to air-fry for 10 minutes.
3. Whisk the yogurt, salt, and dill.
4. Serve the salmon with the sauce with your favorite sides.

Per serving: Calories: 340kcal; Fat: 16g; Carbs: 5g; Protein: 32g

106. Cajun Salmon

Preparation time: 5 minutes

Cooking time: 10 minutes

Servings: 2

Ingredients:

- Salmon fillet (1 - 7 oz.) 0.75-inches thick
- Cajun seasoning
- Juice (¼ of a lemon)

- Optional: Sprinkle of sugar

Directions:

1. Set the Air Fryer at 356⁰ Fahrenheit to preheat for five minutes.
2. Rinse and dry the salmon with a paper towel. Cover the fish with the Cajun coating mix.
3. Place the fillet in the air fryer for seven minutes with the skin side up.
4. Serve with a sprinkle of lemon and a dusting of sugar if desired.

Per serving: Calories: 285kcal; Fat: 17.8g; Carbs: 6.8g; Protein: 42.1g

107. Breaded Cod Sticks

Preparation time: 5 minutes

Cooking time: 20 minutes

Servings: 4

Ingredients:

- Large eggs (2)
- Milk (3 tbsp.)
- Breadcrumbs (2 cups)
- Almond flour (1 cup)
- Cod (1 lb.)

Directions:

1. Heat the Air Fryer to 350⁰ Fahrenheit.
2. Prepare three bowls; one with the milk and eggs, one with the breadcrumbs (salt and pepper if desired), and another with almond flour.
3. Dip the sticks in the flour, egg mixture, and breadcrumbs.

4. Place in the basket and set the timer for 12 minutes. Toss the basket halfway through the cooking process.

5. Serve with your favorite sauce.

Per serving: Calories: 254kcal; Fat: 14.2g; Carbs: 5.7g; Protein: 39.1g

108. Mussels With Pepper

Preparation time: 15 minutes
Cooking time: 20 minutes
Servings: 5
Ingredients:

- 700g mussels
- 1 clove garlic
- 1 tsp oil
- Pepper to taste
- Parsley Taste

Directions:

1. Clean and scrape the mold cover and remove the byssus (the "beard" that comes from the mold).

2. Pour the oil, and clean the mussels and the crushed garlic in the air fryer basket. Set the temperature to 2000C and simmer for 12 minutes.

3. Towards the end of cooking, add black pepper and chopped parsley.

4. Finally, distribute the mussel juice well at the bottom of the basket, stirring the basket.

Per serving: Calories: 150kcal; Fat: 8g; Carbs: 2g; Protein: 15g

109. Monkfish With Olives And Capers

Preparation time: 25 minutes
Cooking time: 40 minutes
Servings: 4
Ingredients:

- 1 monkfish
- 10 cherry tomatoes
- 50 g cailletier olives
- 5 capers

Directions:

1. Spread aluminum foil inside the air fryer basket and place the monkfish clean and skinless.

2. Add chopped tomatoes, olives, capers, oil, and salt.

3. Set the temperature to 1600C.

4. Cook the monkfish for about 40 minutes.

Per serving: Calories: 404kcal; Fat: 29g; Carbs: 36g; Protein: 24g

110. Tuna Fish With White Beans

Preparation time: 6 minutes
Cooking time: 10 minutes
Servings: 1
Ingredients:

- 1 tbsp. olive oil
- 2 tbsp. garlic (minced)
- 2 cups spinach
- 2 tomatoes
- 3 cups white beans
- Salt and pepper to taste
- 1 can of tuna fish

- Cheese to garnish

Directions:

1. Add oil into the air fryer pot.
2. Mix garlic and spinach.
3. Add tomatoes, white beans, and salt and pepper.
4. Cook at 300 deg. F for 10 minutes.
5. When ready, garnish with cheese and serve!

Per serving: Calories: 100kcal; Fat: 10g; Carbs: 8g; Protein: 11g

CHAPTER 10: Dessert Recipes

111. French Toast Bites

Preparation time: 5 minutes

Cooking time: 15 minutes

Servings: 8

Ingredients:

- Almond milk
- Cinnamon
- Sweetener
- 3 eggs
- 4 pieces of wheat bread

Directions:

1. Preheat the air fryer oven to 360 degrees.
2. Whisk eggs and thin out with almond milk.
3. Mix 1/3 cup of sweetener with lots of cinnamon.
4. Tear bread in half, ball up pieces and press them together to form a ball.
5. Soak bread balls in egg and then roll into cinnamon sugar, thoroughly coat.
6. Place coated bread balls into the air fryer oven and bake for 15 minutes.

Per serving: Calories: 289kcal; Fat: 11g; Carbs: 17g; Protein: 0g

112. Berry Yogurt Cake

Preparation time: 15 minutes

Cooking time: 60 minutes

Servings: 12

Ingredients:

- 2 eggs
- 1 lemon
- 1 cup of berries
- 1/2 tsp of salt
- 1 1/2 tsp of baking powder
- 1 1/2 cups of cake flour
- 1/4 tsp of baking soda
- 1 cup of brown sugar
- 1/2 tsp of vanilla extract
- 1/2 cup of olive oil
- 1/2 cup of Greek yogurt
- 3 tbsp of lemon juice

Directions:

1. Add all the ingredients except baking powder, soda, salt, and flour to a separate bowl and whisk together until smooth.
2. Then combine the salt, baking powder, soda, and flour.
3. Add olive oil and whisk until well combined.
4. Add mixed berries. Preheat the air fryer to 300 deg. F.
5. Grease pan with oil. Add the batter to it.
6. Cook in the air fryer for about 60 minutes.
7. Then, slice and serve.

Per serving: Calories: 291kcal; Fat: 10g; Carbs: 44g; Protein: 5g

113. Cinnamon Sugar Roasted Chickpeas

Preparation time: 5 minutes

Cooking time: 10 minutes

Servings: 2

Ingredients:

- 1 tbsp. sweetener
- 1 tbsp. cinnamon
- 1 C. chickpeas

Directions:

1. Preheat the air fryer oven to 390 degrees.
2. Rinse and drain chickpeas.
3. Mix all ingredients and add to the air fryer.
4. Pour into the Oven rack/basket. Place the Rack on the middle shelf of the Air fryer oven. Set temperature to 390 deg. F, and set the time to 10 minutes.

Per serving: Calories: 111kcal; Fat: 19g; Carbs: 18g; Protein: 16g

114. Honey Fruit Compote

Preparation time: 10 minutes

Cooking time: 3 minutes

Servings: 4

Ingredients:

- 1/3 cup honey
- 1 1/2 cups blueberries
- 1 1/2 cups raspberries

Directions:

1. Put all of the ingredients in the air fryer basket and stir well.

2. Seal pot with lid and cook on high for 3 minutes.
3. Once done, allow to release of pressure naturally. Remove lid.
4. Serve and enjoy.

Per serving: Calories: 141kcal; Fat: 0.5g; Carbs: 36.7g; Protein: 1g

115. Pumpkin Cupcakes

Preparation time: 20 minutes

Cooking time: 12 minutes

Servings: 10

Ingredients:

- 3 eggs
- 1 can of pumpkin puree
- 1/4 tsp of cinnamon
- 1 box of spice cake mix
- 1/2 cup of vegetable oil
- 1 tsp of pumpkin pie spice
- 2 cans of cream cheese

Directions:

1. Combine all ingredients in a bowl. Line molds with cooking spray and parchment paper.
2. Fill molds full with batter.
3. Place them in the air fryer and cook for about 12 minutes at 320°F.
4. Once done, let them cool.
5. Make the icing by mixing cinnamon and cream cheese.
6. Pour in an icing bag. Keep in the fridge for about 5 minutes.
7. Then top the cupcakes with icing. Serve and enjoy.

Per serving: Calories: 225kcal; Fat: 10g; Carbs: 31g; Protein: 3g

116. Peach Cobbler Bites

Preparation time: 10 minutes

Cooking time: 8 minutes

Servings: 2

Ingredients:

- Salt
- 1 peach
- 1/4 cup of egg whites
- 1/4 tsp of vanilla extract
- 1/4 cup of breadcrumbs
- 1 pack of natural sweetener
- 1/4 tsp of cinnamon

Directions:

1. Cut peach into equal slices.
2. Mix salt, sweetener, cinnamon, and breadcrumbs in a bowl.
3. Mix egg and vanilla extract in a separate bowl.
4. Coat peach slices with it. Then, coat in the breadcrumb mix.
5. Spray some oil on the air fryer basket.
6. Put them in the air fryer.
7. Cook at 392 deg. F for about 8 minutes. Enjoy.

Per serving: Calories: 144kcal; Fat: 0.5g; Carbs: 28.5g; Protein: 6g

117. Plum Apple Tarts

Preparation time: 10 minutes

Cooking time: 8 minutes

Servings: 4

Ingredients:

- 2 plums
- 1 apple
- 1 egg
- 1 sheet of puff pastry
- 1 tbsp of lemon juice
- 1 tsp of cinnamon
- 3 tbsp of brown sugar
- 1 tbsp of icing sugar

Directions:

1. Slice apple and plums.
2. Mix fruits, brown sugar, lemon juice, and cinnamon in a bowl.
3. Cut circles out of pastry sheets.
4. Add filling in the center.
5. Brush egg washes on sides and fold. Set the air fryer to 330°F.
6. Cook these tarts for about 8 minutes.
7. Sprinkle powdered sugar on top. Serve and enjoy.

Per serving: Calories: 143kcal; Fat: 4g; Carbs: 26g; Protein: 3g

118. Spiced Pear Sauce

Preparation time: 10 minutes

Cooking time: 6 hours

Servings: 12

Ingredients:

- 8 pears, cored and diced

- 1/2 tsp ground cinnamon
- 1/4 tsp ground nutmeg
- 1/4 tsp ground cardamom
- 1 cup of water

Directions:

1. Put all of the ingredients in the air fryer and stir well.
2. Seal the pot with a lid, select slow cook mode, and cook on low for 6 hours.
3. Mash the sauce using a potato masher.
4. Pour into the container and store.

Per serving: Calories: 81kcal; Fat: 0.2g; Carbs: 21.4g; Protein: 0.5g

119. Apple Dumplings

Preparation time: 10 minutes
Cooking time: 25 minutes
Servings: 4
Ingredients:

- 2 tbsp. melted coconut oil
- 2 puff pastry sheets
- 1 tbsp. brown sugar
- 2 tbsp. raisins
- 2 small apples of choice

Directions:

1. Ensure your air fryer oven is preheated to 356 degrees.
2. Core and peel apples and mix with raisins and sugar.

3. Place a bit of apple mixture into puff pastry sheets and brush the sides with melted coconut oil.
4. Place into the air fryer. Cook for 25 minutes, turning halfway through. It will be golden when done.

Per serving: Calories: 367kcal; Fat: 7g; Carbs: 10g; Protein: 2g

120. Apple Hand Pies

Preparation time: 5 minutes
Cooking time: 8 minutes
Servings: 6
Ingredients:

- 15-ounces no-sugar-added apple pie filling
- 1 store-bought crust

Directions:

1. Lay out the pie crust and slice it into equal-sized squares.
2. Place 2 tbsp. filling into each square and sealing the crust with a fork.
3. Pour into the Oven rack/basket. Place the Rack on the middle shelf of the Air fryer oven.
4. Set temperature to 390 deg. F, and set time to 8 minutes until golden in color.

Per serving: Calories: 278kcal; Fat: 10g; Carbs: 17g; Protein: 5g

30-Day Meal Plan

Days	Breakfast	Lunch	Dinner	Dessert
1	Cheesy Red Bean Soup	Tomato Soup	Taco Cheese Soup	Coconut Lime Soup
2	Healthy Bean Soup	Mushrooms Mix Veg Broth	Air Fryer Vegetable Soup	Roasted Tomato Soup
3	Air Fryer Fish Stew	Kale Cottage Cheese Soup	Carrot Soup With Fowl	Basil Tomato Soup
4	Air Fryer Greek Beef Stew	Pepper Beef Stew	Chicken Rice Noodle Soup	Tortilla And White Beans Soup
5	Onion Soup	Kale Beef Soup	Asian Pork Soup	Air Fryer Bean Soup
6	Healthy Bean Soup	Tomato Soup	Kale Cottage Cheese Soup	Coconut Lime Soup
7	Kale Cottage Cheese Soup	Air Fryer Vegetable Soup	Onion Soup	Roasted Tomato Soup
8	Mushrooms Mix Veg Broth	Air Fryer Greek Beef Stew	Tortilla And White Beans Soup	Kale Beef Soup
9	Tortilla And White Beans Soup	Pepper Beef Stew	Basil Tomato Soup	Air Fryer Vegetable Soup
10	Chicken Rice Noodle Soup	Asian Pork Soup	Cheesy Red Bean Soup	Asian Pork Soup
11	Carrot Soup With Fowl	Carrot Soup With Fowl	Roasted Tomato Soup	Taco Cheese Soup
12	Air Fryer Bean Soup	Air Fryer Fish Stew	Coconut Lime Soup	Mushrooms Mix Veg Broth
13	Healthy Bean Soup	Air Fryer Greek Beef Stew	Cheesy Red Bean Soup	Air Fryer Fish Stew
14	Basil Tomato Soup	Pepper Beef Stew	Chicken Rice Noodle Soup	Air Fryer Bean Soup

15	Simple Egg Breakfast	Creamy Cabbage	Avocados With Cilantro	Pumpkin Cupcakes
16	Air Fried Banana Bites	Herbed Tomatoes	Soft Tofu With Veggies	Apple Dumplings
17	Muffin Mix Breakfast	Veg Buffalo Cauliflower	Salty Lemon Artichokes	Berry Yogurt Cake
18	Eggs With Dill	Cheesy Roasted Eggplants	Onion Green Beans	French Toast Bites
19	Lemony Raspberries Bowls	Lemony Baby Potatoes	Zucchini Squash Mix	Plum Apple Tarts
20	Apple Pie	Mushrooms With Veggies And Avocado	Creamy Zucchini And Sweet Potatoes	Peach Cobbler Bites
21	Tuna And Spring Onions Salad	Herbed Tomatoes With Jalapeno	Endives With Seitan Mix	Honey Fruit Compote
22	Kale With Tuna	Spiced Almonds	Almond Flour Battered And Crisped Onion Rings	Apple Hand Pies
23	Breakfast Fish Tacos	Flatbread	Chard With Cheddar	Cinnamon Sugar Roasted Chickpeas
24	Garlic Potatoes With Bacon	Green Beans And Cherry Tomatoes	Simple Haddock	Plum Apple Tarts
25	Mushrooms And Cheese Spread	Avocados With Cilantro	Endives With Seitan Mix	Berry Yogurt Cake
26	Protein Egg Cups	Veg Buffalo Cauliflower	Herbed Tomatoes With Jalapeno	Honey Fruit Compote
27	Shrimp Frittata	Mushrooms With Veggies And Avocado	Green Beans And Cherry Tomatoes	Peach Cobbler Bites

28	Garlic Bacon Pizza	Creamy Zucchini And Sweet Potatoes	Lemony Baby Potatoes	Apple Dumplings
29	Almond Crust Chicken	Garlic Chicken Wings	Korean Beef	Cinnamon Sugar Roasted Chickpeas
30	Asparagus Salad	Cod Fish Nuggets	Cornish Chicken	Spiced Pear Sauce

Conversion Chart

Volume Equivalents (Liquid)

US Standard	US Standard (ounces)	Metric (approximate)
2 tablespoons	1 fl. oz.	30 mL
¼ cup	2 fl. oz.	60 mL
½ cup	4 fl. oz.	120 mL
1 cup	8 fl. oz.	240 mL
1½ cups	12 fl. oz.	355 mL
2 cups or 1 pint	16 fl. oz.	475 mL
4 cups or 1 quart	32 fl. oz.	1 L
1 gallon	128 fl. oz.	4 L

Volume Equivalents (Dry)

US Standard	Metric (approximate)
⅛ teaspoon	0.5 mL
¼ teaspoon	1 mL
½ teaspoon	2 mL
¾ teaspoon	4 mL
1 teaspoon	5 mL
1 tablespoon	15 mL
¼ cup	59 mL
⅓ cup	79 mL

½ cup	118 mL
⅔ cup	156 mL
¾ cup	177 mL
1 cup	235 mL
2 cups or 1 pint	475 mL
3 cups	700 mL
4 cups or 1 quart	1 L

Oven Temperatures

Fahrenheit (F)	Celsius (C) (approximate)
250°F	120°C
300°F	150°C
325°F	165°C
350°F	180°C
375°F	190°C
400°F	200°C
425°F	220°C
450°F	230°C

Weight Equivalents

US Standard	Metric (approximate)
½ ounce	15 g
1 ounce	30 g
2 ounces	60 g
4 ounces	115 g
8 ounces	225 g
12 ounces	340 g
16 ounces or 1 pound	455 g

Conclusion

Bariatric surgery alters how food reaches your intestines by reducing the size of your stomach. Following the treatment, ensuring proper Nutrition: when gaining weight is essential.

Transitioning into a healthier lifestyle that supports your weight-loss goals will take effort with proper meal planning and a versatile tool like the air fryer. Nothing is impossible. An air fryer is a slick gadget that supports the low-fat requirement of a bariatric diet. This kitchen appliance will make delicious and nutritious surgery-safe foods easily and quickly.

The element in the air fryer creates heat and is distributed equally across the appliance by a fan. This is true for each purpose. Whether you're roasting, broiling, or doing something else doesn't matter. When you place the dish on any type of tray and choose the feature, the unit will automatically start and set the temperature. You can adjust it if you like, even though it is fixed automatically

By reducing the size of your stomach, bariatric surgery changes how food enters your intestines. After the procedure, getting adequate nourishment while losing weight is essential.

More people, who have chosen to go on this diet, have started to travel outside their hometowns to find and purchase an air fryer. With the time people spend traveling daily, ensuring that all those snacks and meals are prepared when they get home can be challenging. With this said, you will need to ensure that you know how to cook as much as possible at home before eating out for any of your meals. However, there is another way you can eat at home, and that is with an air fryer.

The convenience of using an air fryer is that you can cook any food without dealing with messy oils and deep-fried foods. Cooking food in the air fryer will also ensure that your food will be evenly cooked so that you won't end up with a burnt patty on one side while the other remains raw. The best part of using an air fryer is that it's straightforward. You need to turn it on and select the desired temperature. The air fryer can be used for various cooking methods such as baking, poaching, roasting, grilling, and frying. Just always remember to preheat your air fryer before adding in the food.

Of course, regular follow-up visits with your surgery team will determine your long-term safety and success. After completing the scheduled appointments during the first year, getting checked annually is recommended.

Index

Onion Mix Tofu Side Dish; 55
Onion Soup; 32
Peach Cobbler Bites; 75
Pepper Beef Stew; 31
Plum Apple Tarts; 75
Potatoes With Bacon; 38
Protein Egg Cups; 40
Pumpkin Cupcakes; 74
Pumpkin Quick Dish; 53
Roasted Tomato Soup; 29
Romesco Sauce; 57
Salami Bites; 64
Salmon With Pistachio Bark; 67
Salted Marinated Salmon; 67
Salty Lemon Artichokes; 49
Sesame Sauce; 59
Shrimp Frittata; 39
Shrimp, Zucchini And Cherry Tomato Sauce; 68

Simple Egg Breakfast; 37
Simple Haddock; 45
Soft Tofu with Veggies; 51
Spiced Almonds; 44
Spiced Pear Sauce; 75
Spinach With Salmon And Seashells; 69
Steak With Cabbage; 63
Sweet Potato Tots; 55
Taco Cheese Soup; 27
Tomato Soup; 26
Tortilla And White Beans Soup; 30
Tuna And Spring Onions Salad; 37
Tuna Fish With White Beans; 71
Turkey Breast; 66
Veg Buffalo Cauliflower; 50
Vegan Mayo Sauce; 59
Whole Wheat Air Fried Pizzas; 53
Zucchini Squash Mix; 47

Made in the USA
Monee, IL
16 January 2024

51881030R00046